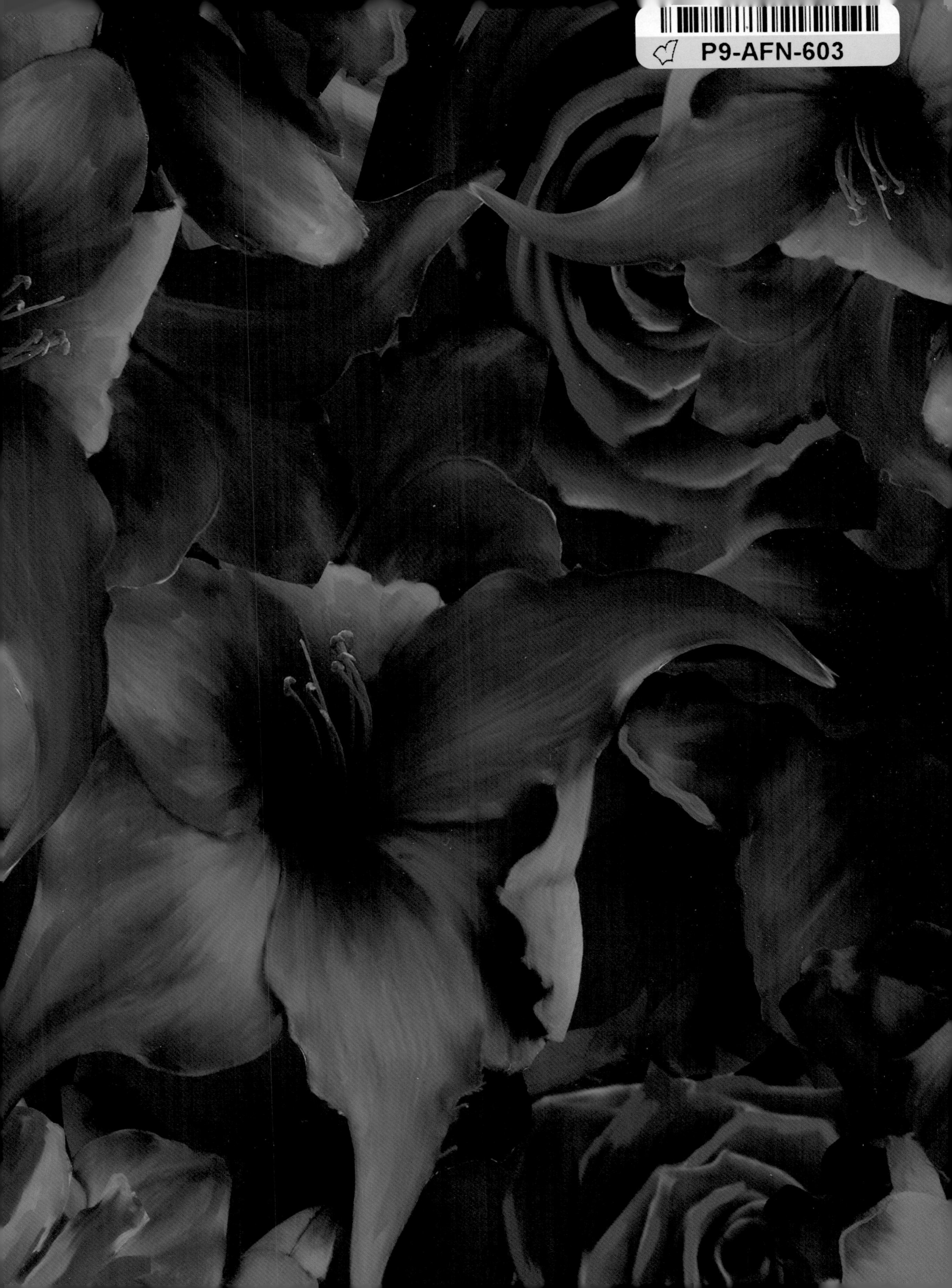

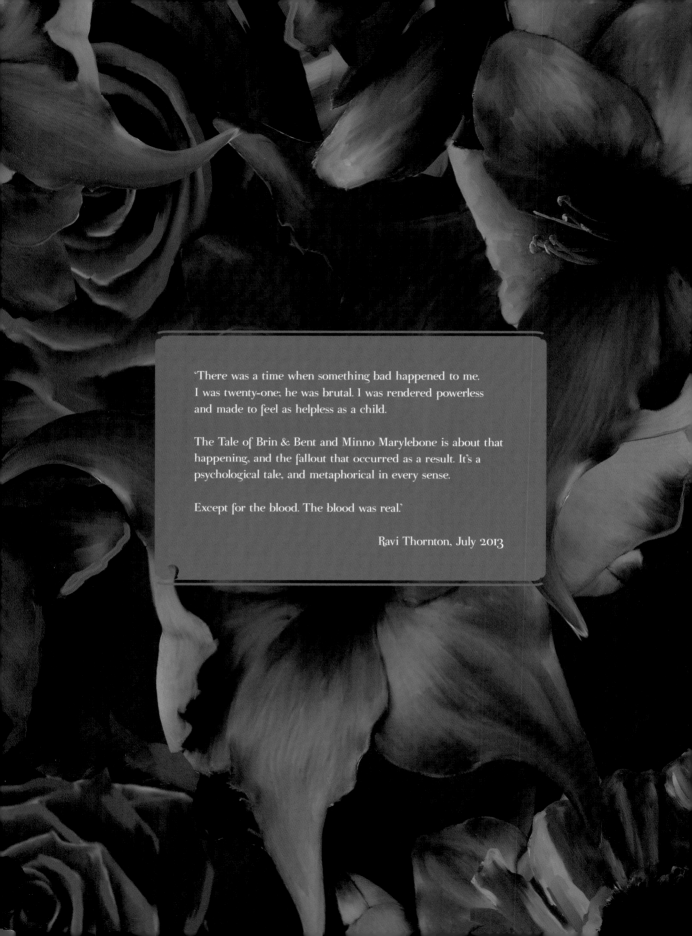

'There was a time when something bad happened to me.
I was twenty-one; he was brutal. I was rendered powerless
and made to feel as helpless as a child.

The Tale of Brin & Bent and Minno Marylebone is about that
happening, and the fallout that occurred as a result. It's a
psychological tale, and metaphorical in every sense.

Except for the blood. The blood was real.'

Ravi Thornton, July 2013

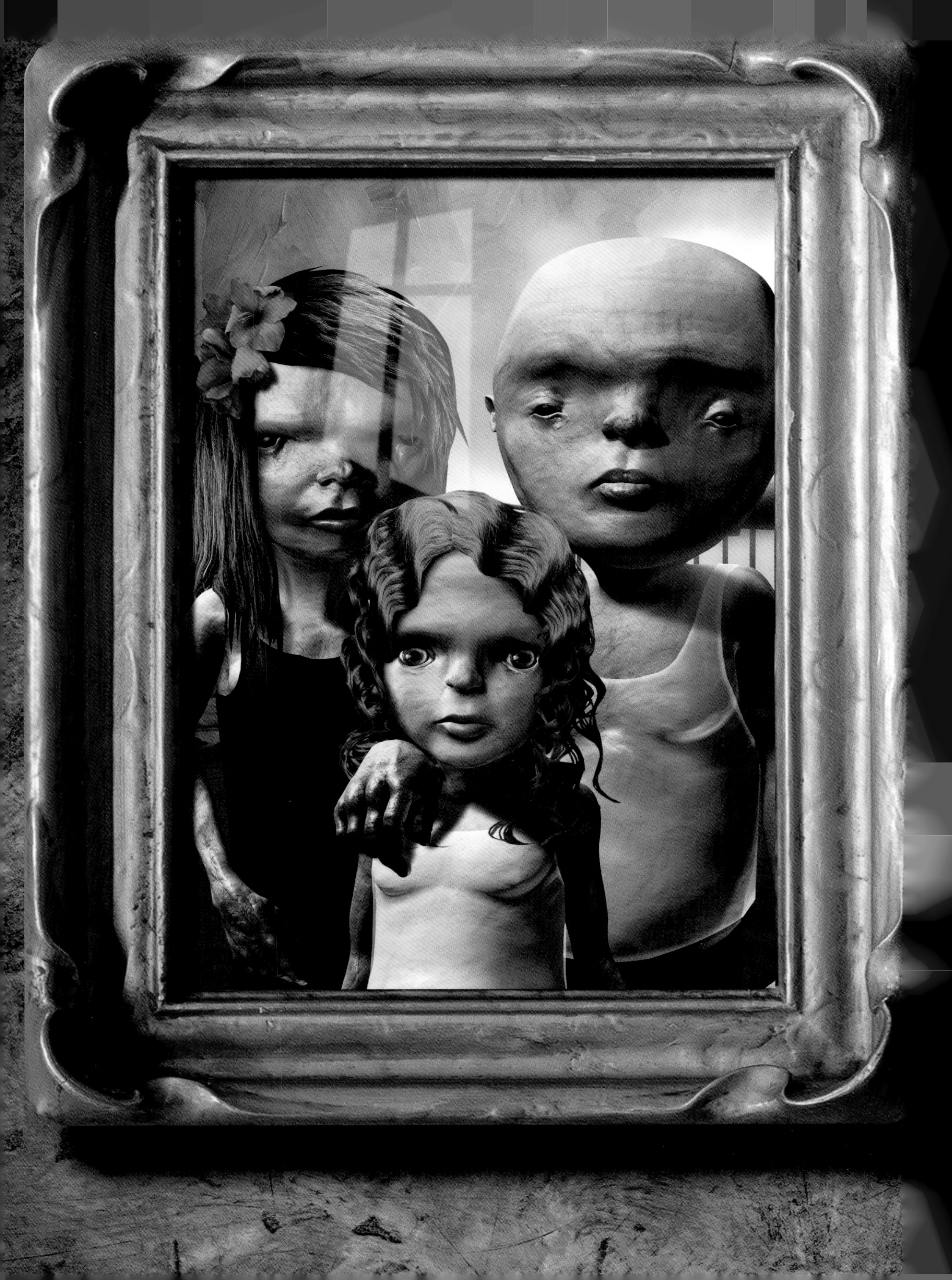

There stands The House of Care for the Grossly Infirm.

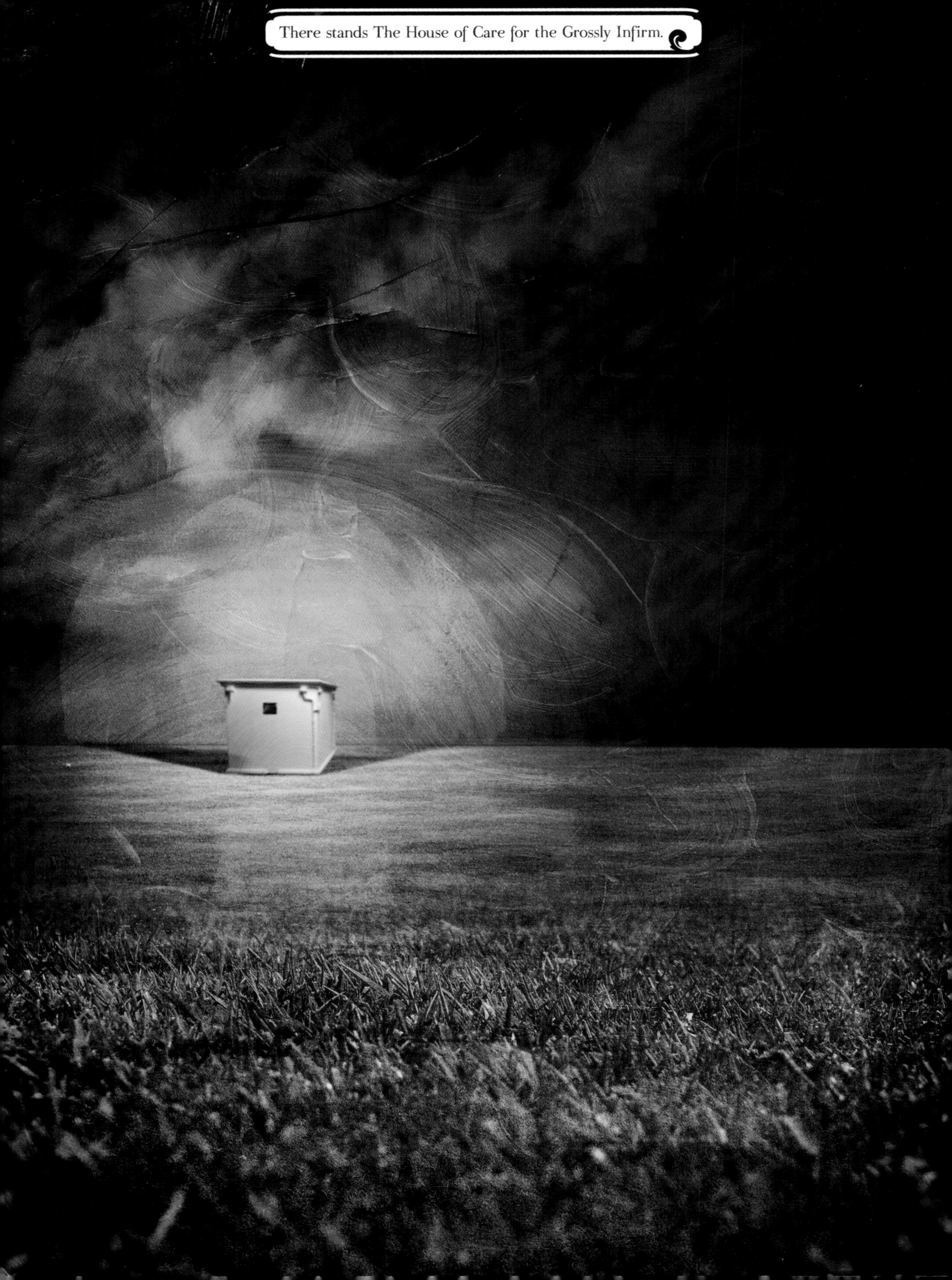

THE TALE OF BRIN & BENT AND MINNO MARYLEBON

WRITTEN BY
RAVI THORNTON

ILLUSTRATED BY
ANDY HIXON

TITLES BY
STEPHEN NUTTALL

SOFT SKULL PRESS | An imprint of COUNTERPOINT | BERKELEY

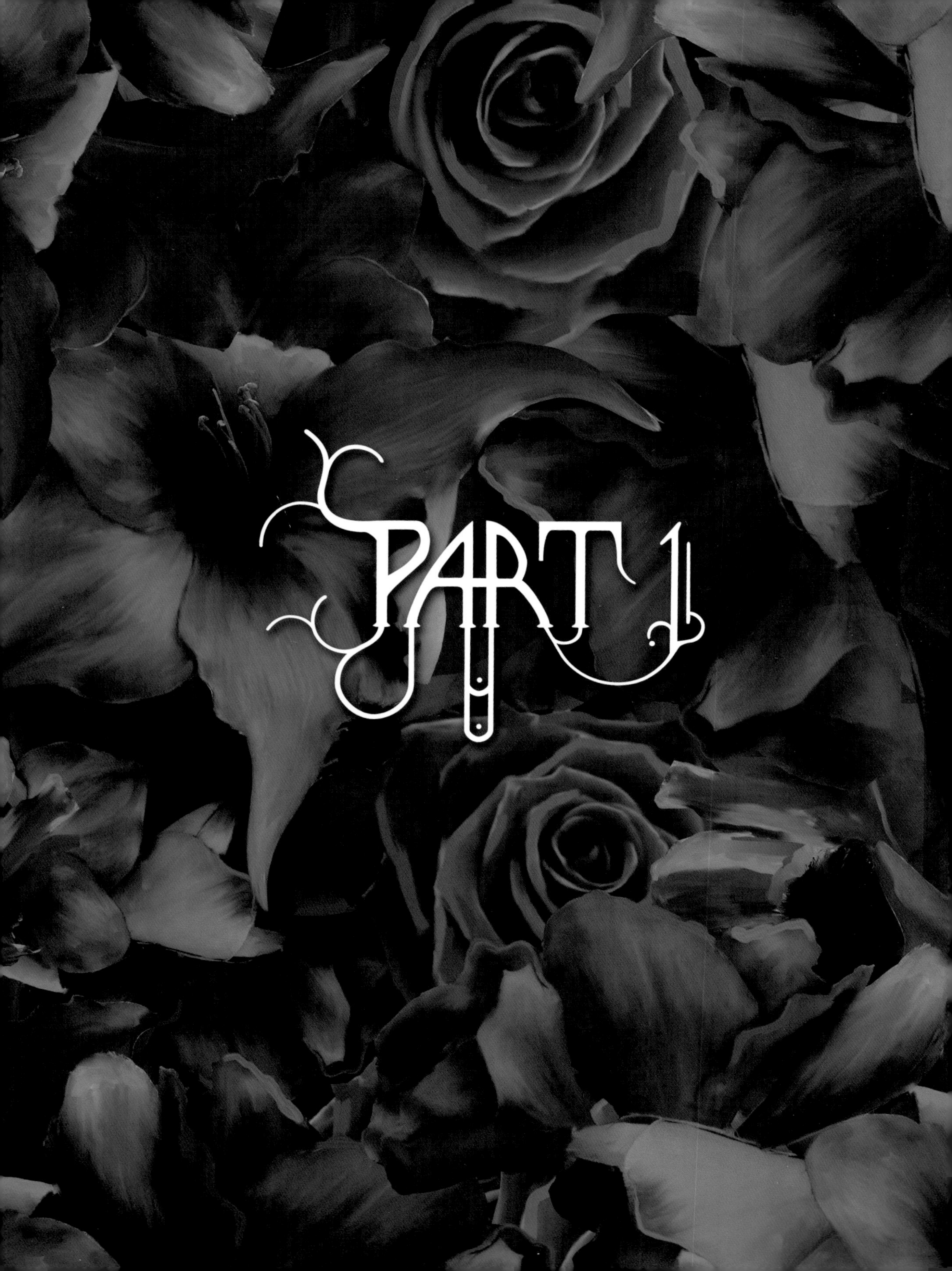

PART 1

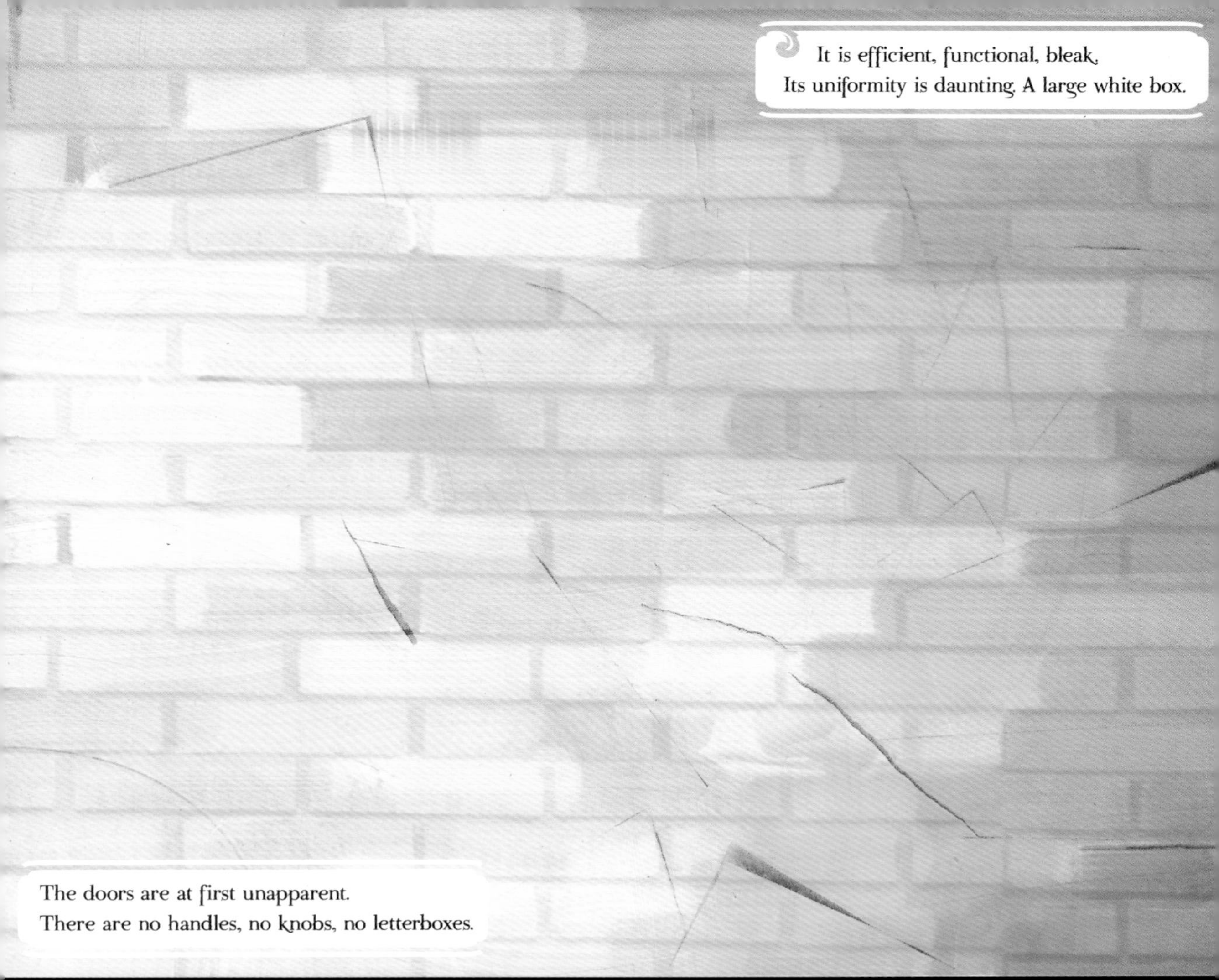
It is efficient, functional, bleak.
Its uniformity is daunting. A large white box.
The doors are at first unapparent.
There are no handles, no knobs, no letterboxes.

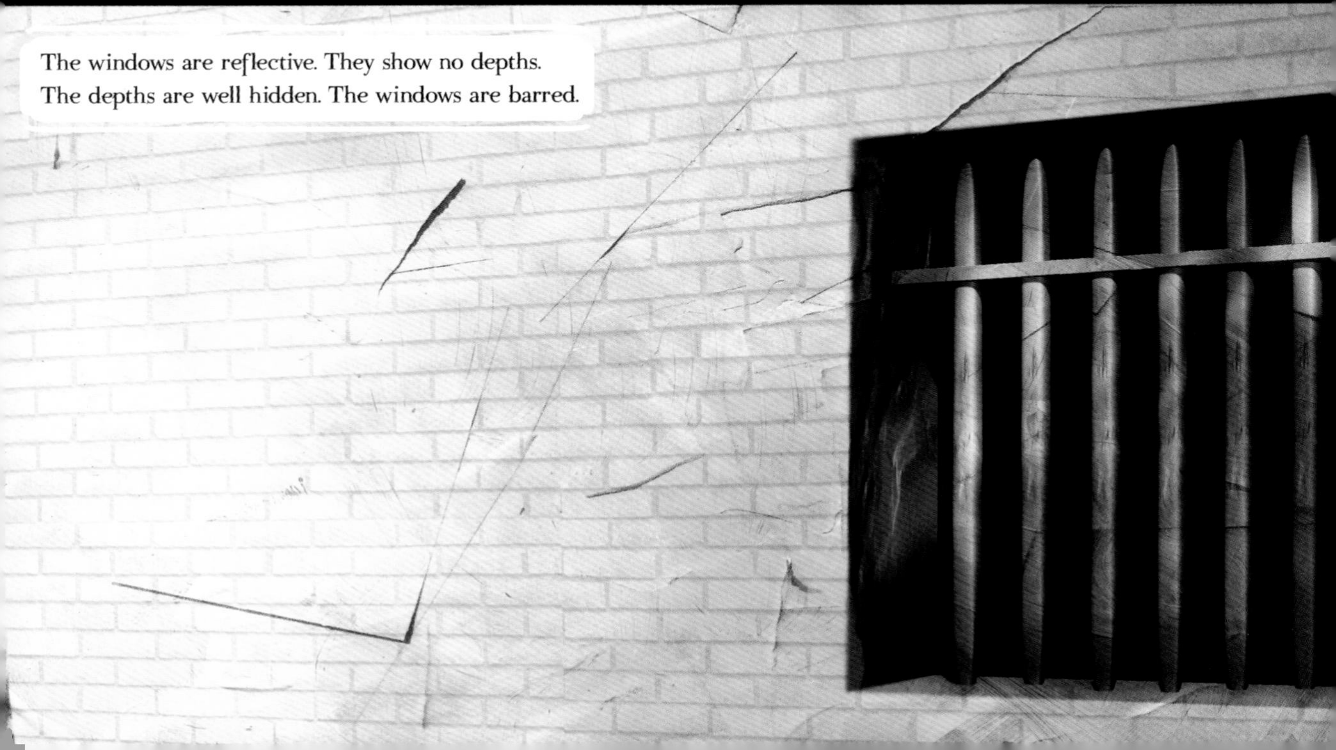
The windows are reflective. They show no depths.
The depths are well hidden. The windows are barred.

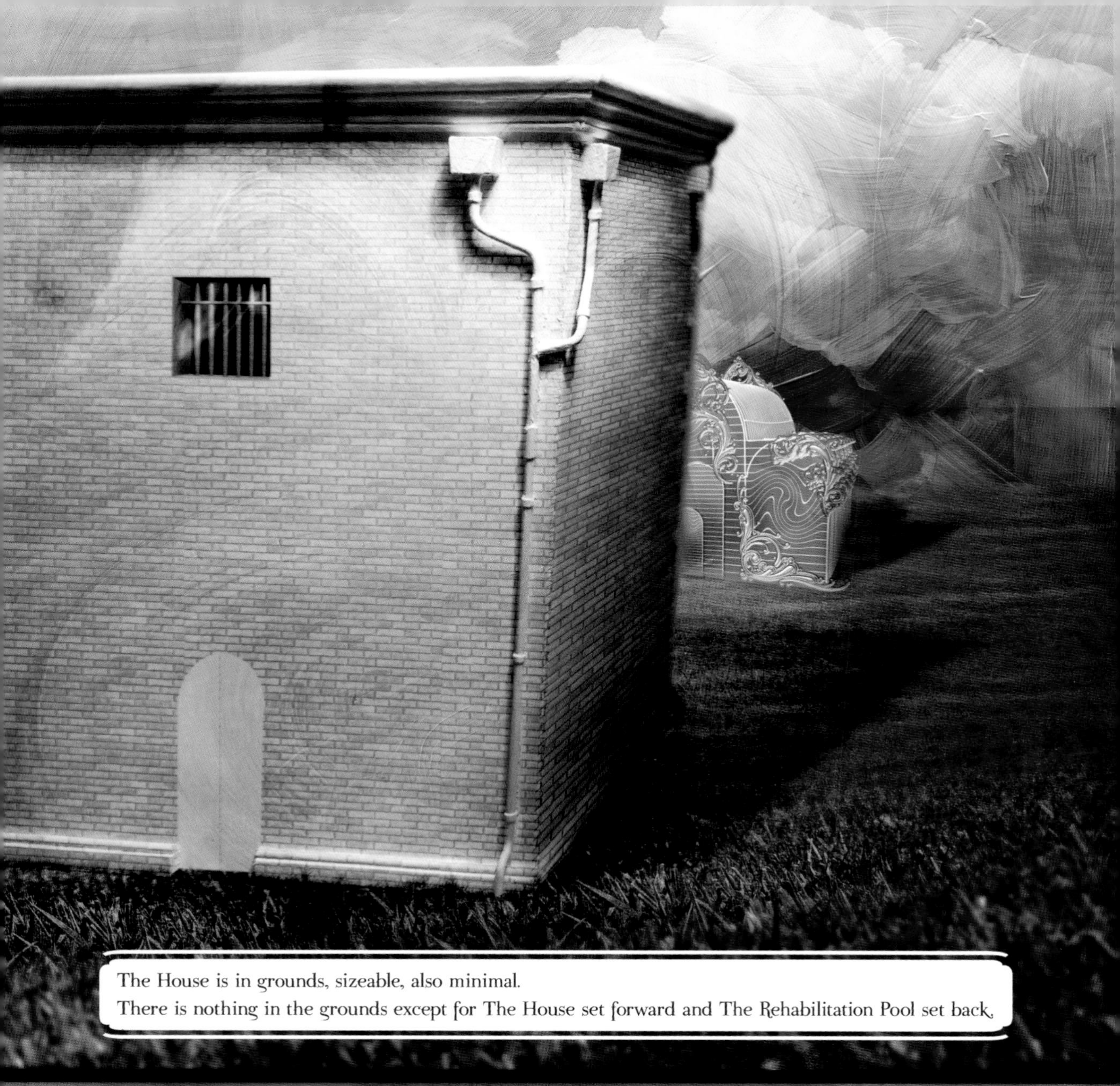
The House is in grounds, sizeable, also minimal.
There is nothing in the grounds except for The House set forward and The Rehabilitation Pool set back.

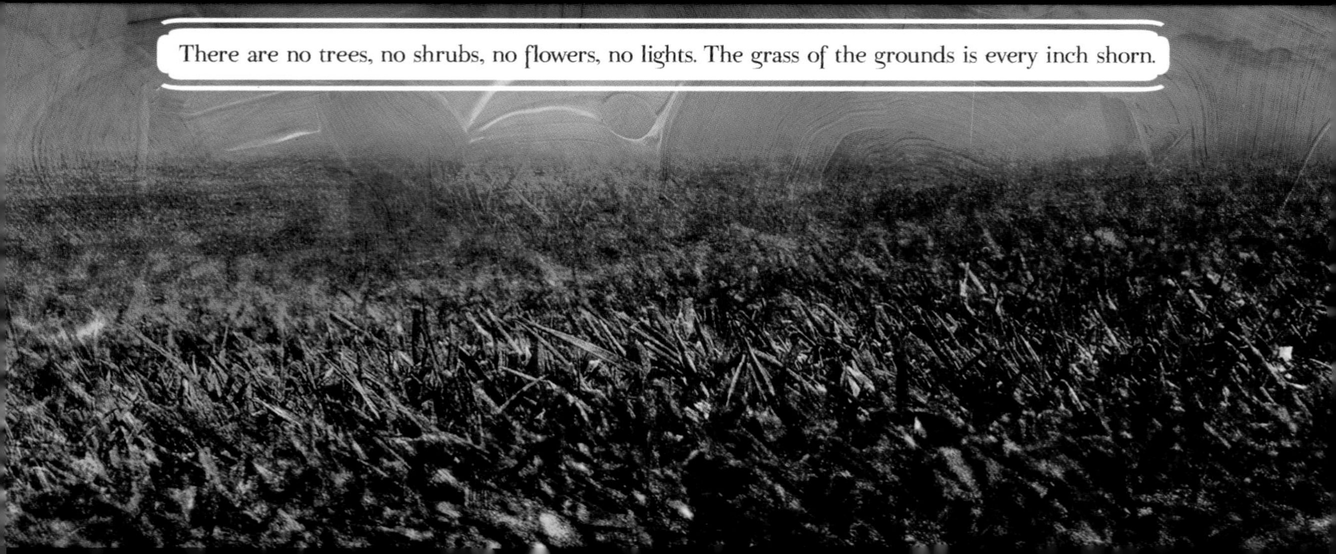
There are no trees, no shrubs, no flowers, no lights. The grass of the grounds is every inch shorn.

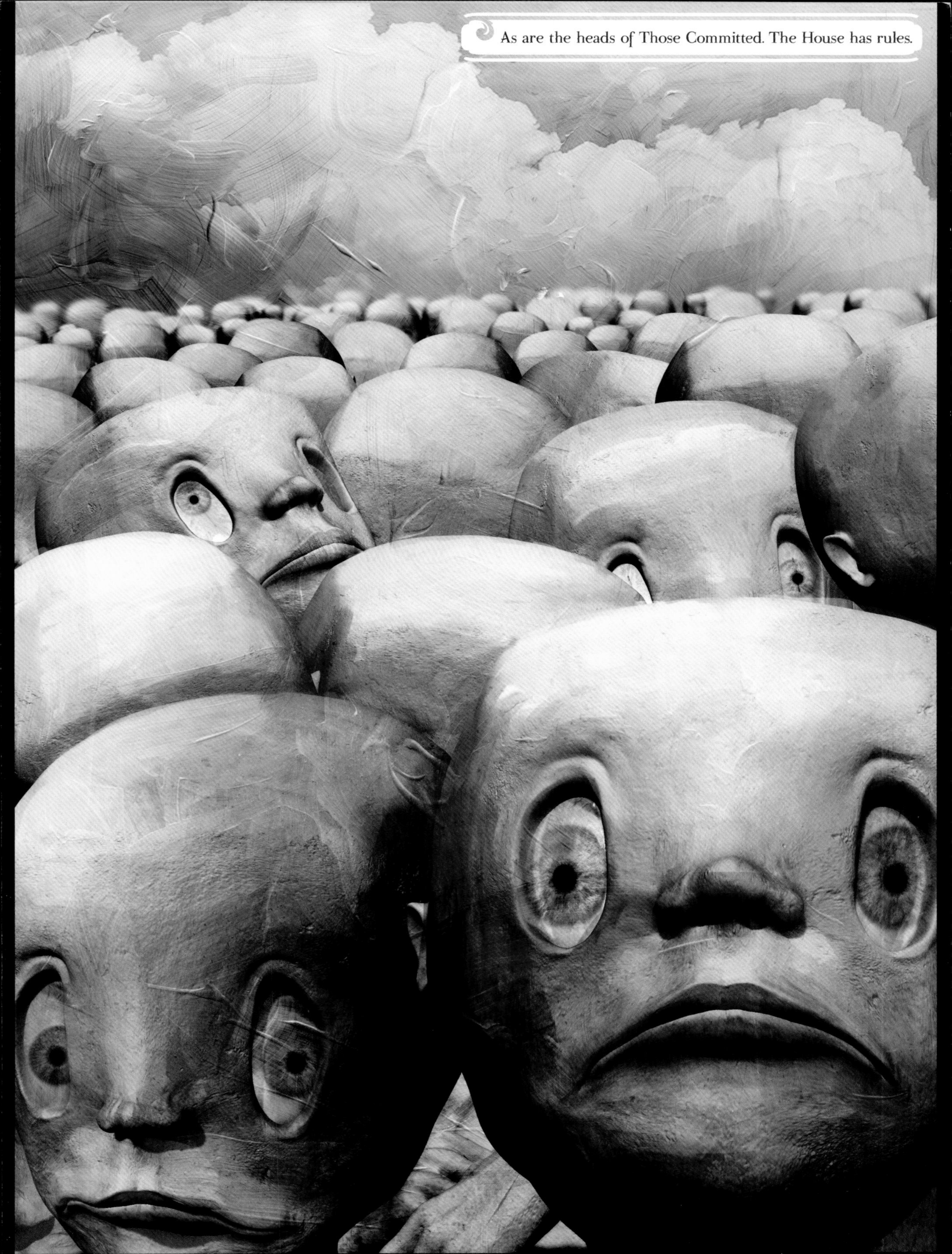

As are the heads of Those Committed. The House has rules.

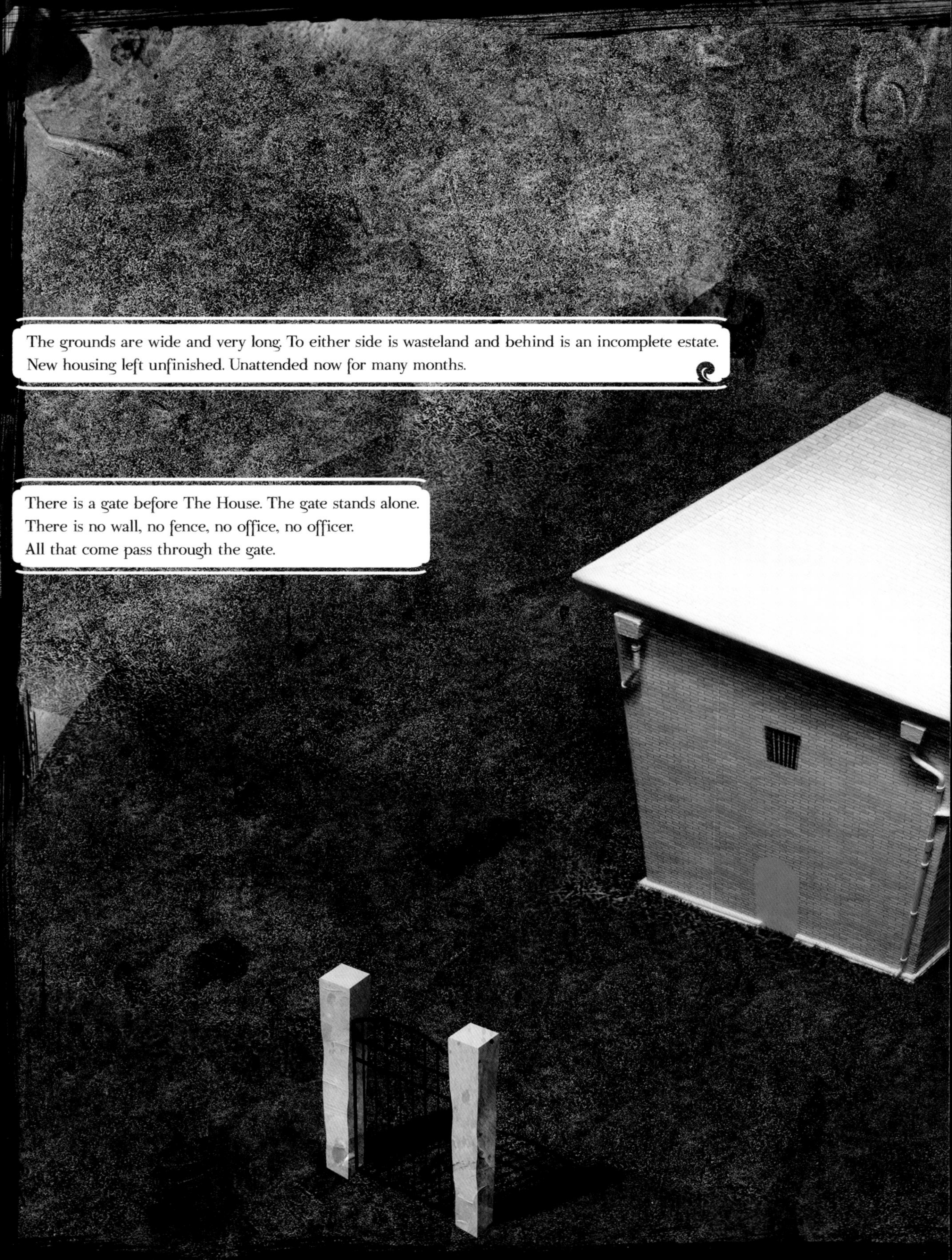
The grounds are wide and very long. To either side is wasteland and behind is an incomplete estate. New housing left unfinished. Unattended now for many months.
There is a gate before The House. The gate stands alone.
There is no wall, no fence, no office, no officer.
All that come pass through the gate.

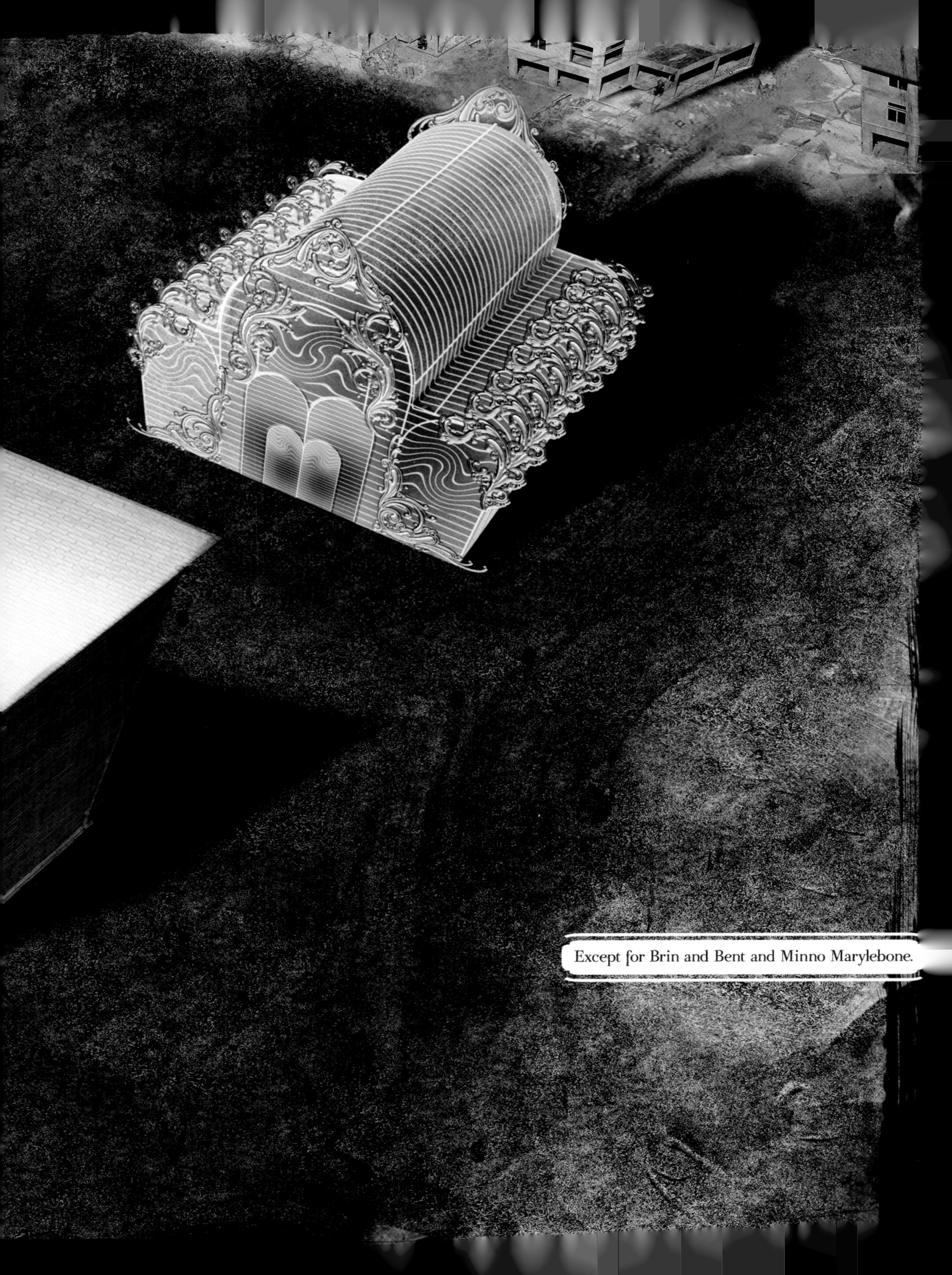
Except for Brin and Bent and Minno Marylebone.

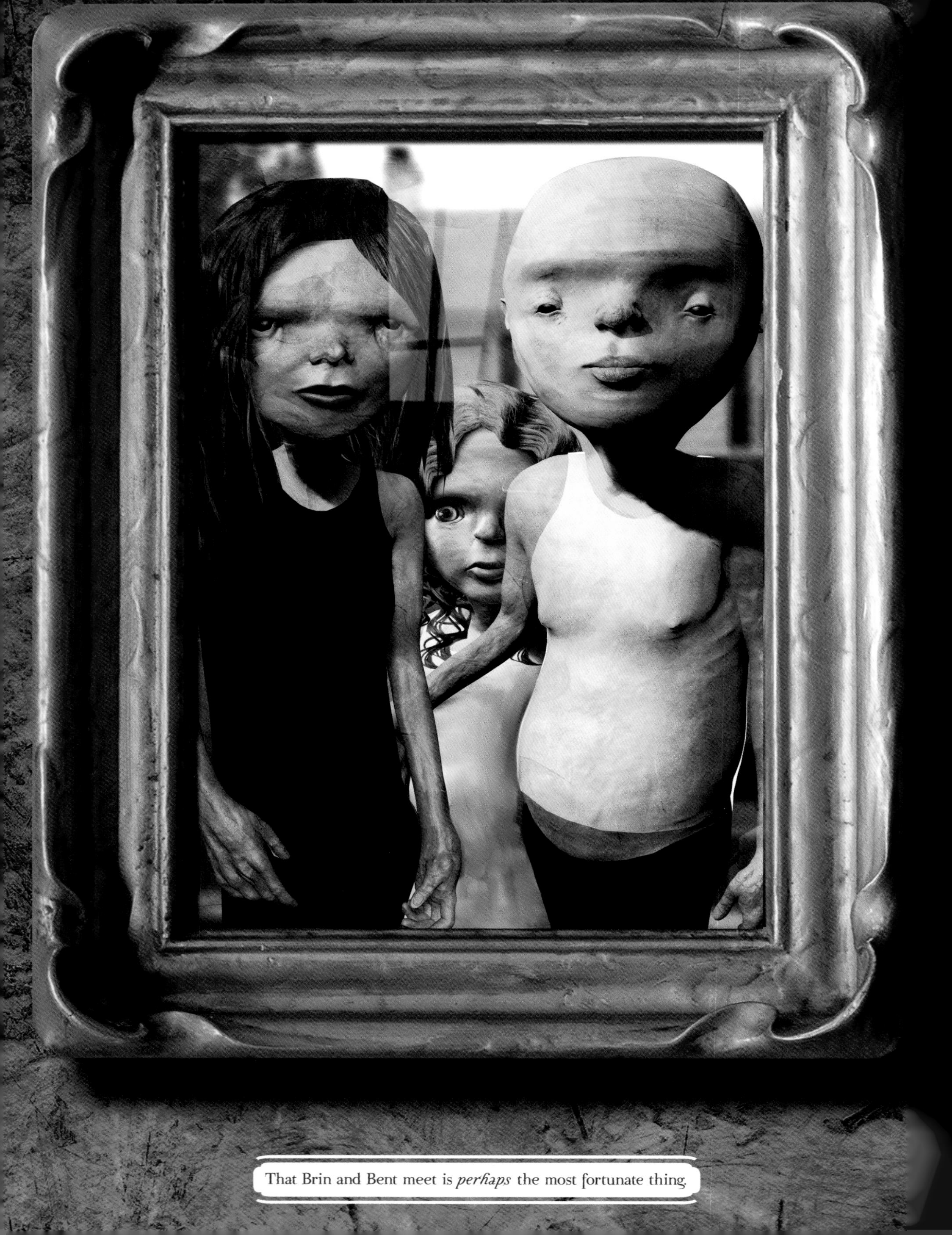

That Brin and Bent meet is *perhaps* the most fortunate thing.

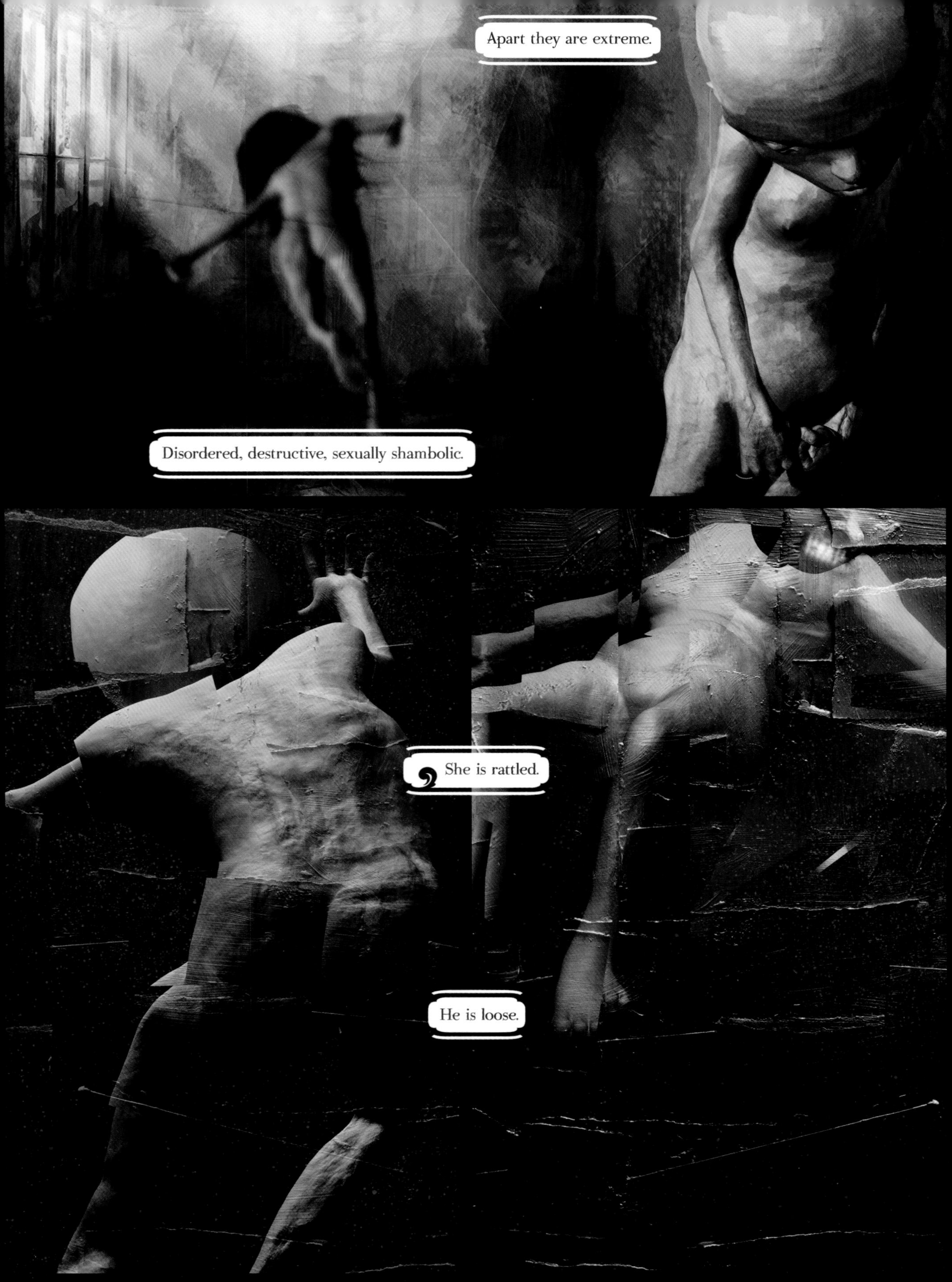
Apart they are extreme.
Disordered, destructive, sexually shambolic.
She is rattled.
He is loose.

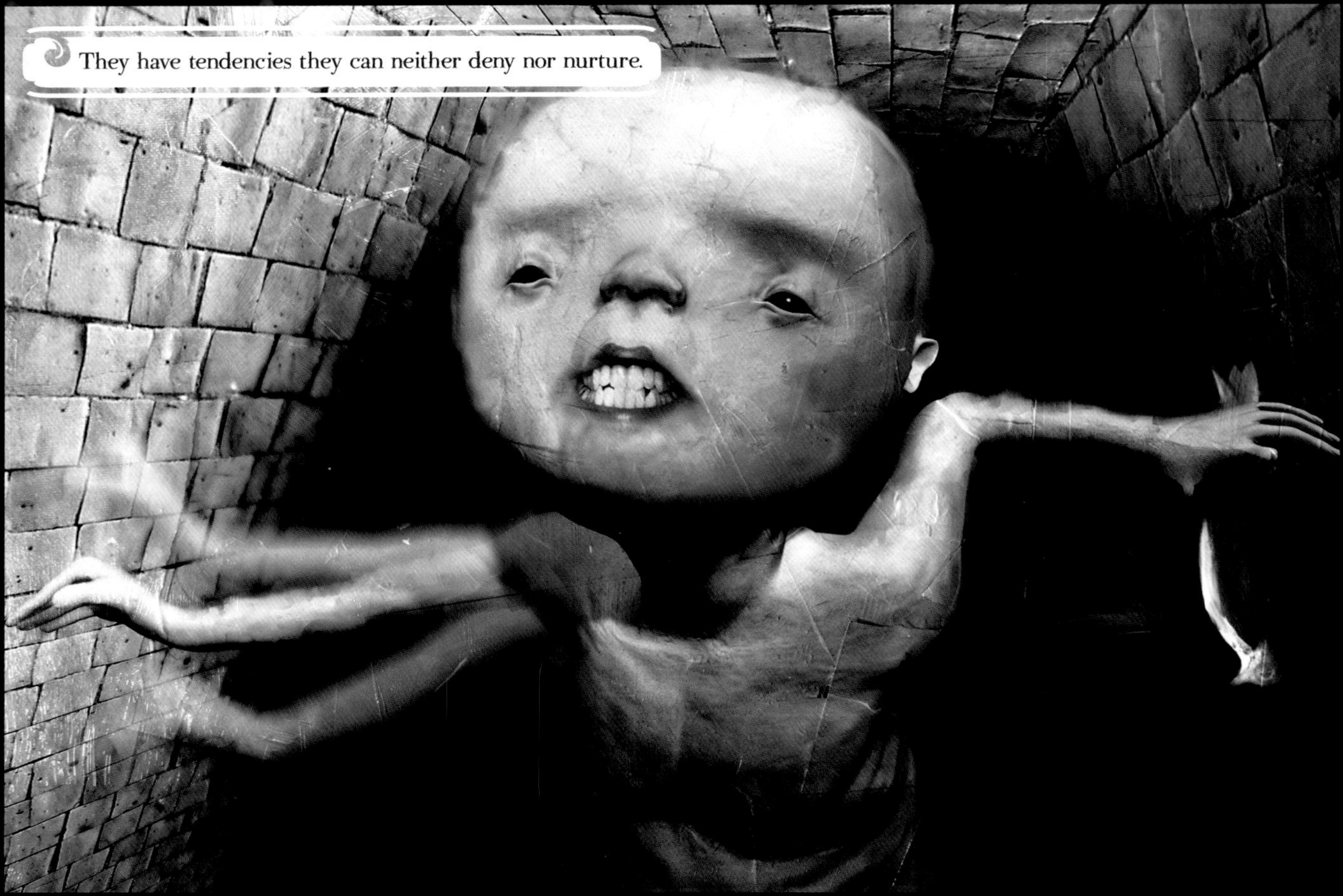
They have tendencies they can neither deny nor nurture.

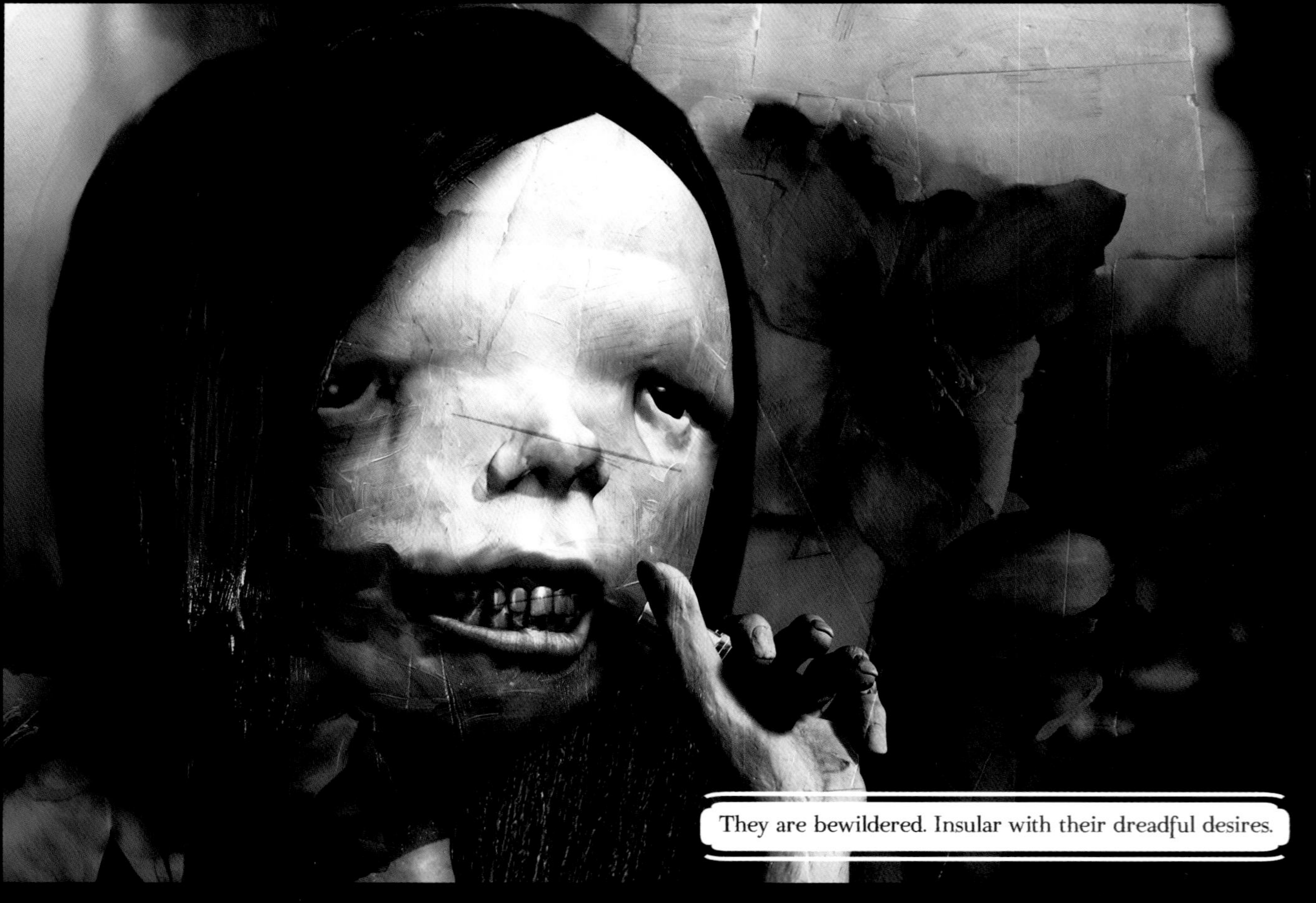
They are bewildered. Insular with their dreadful desires.

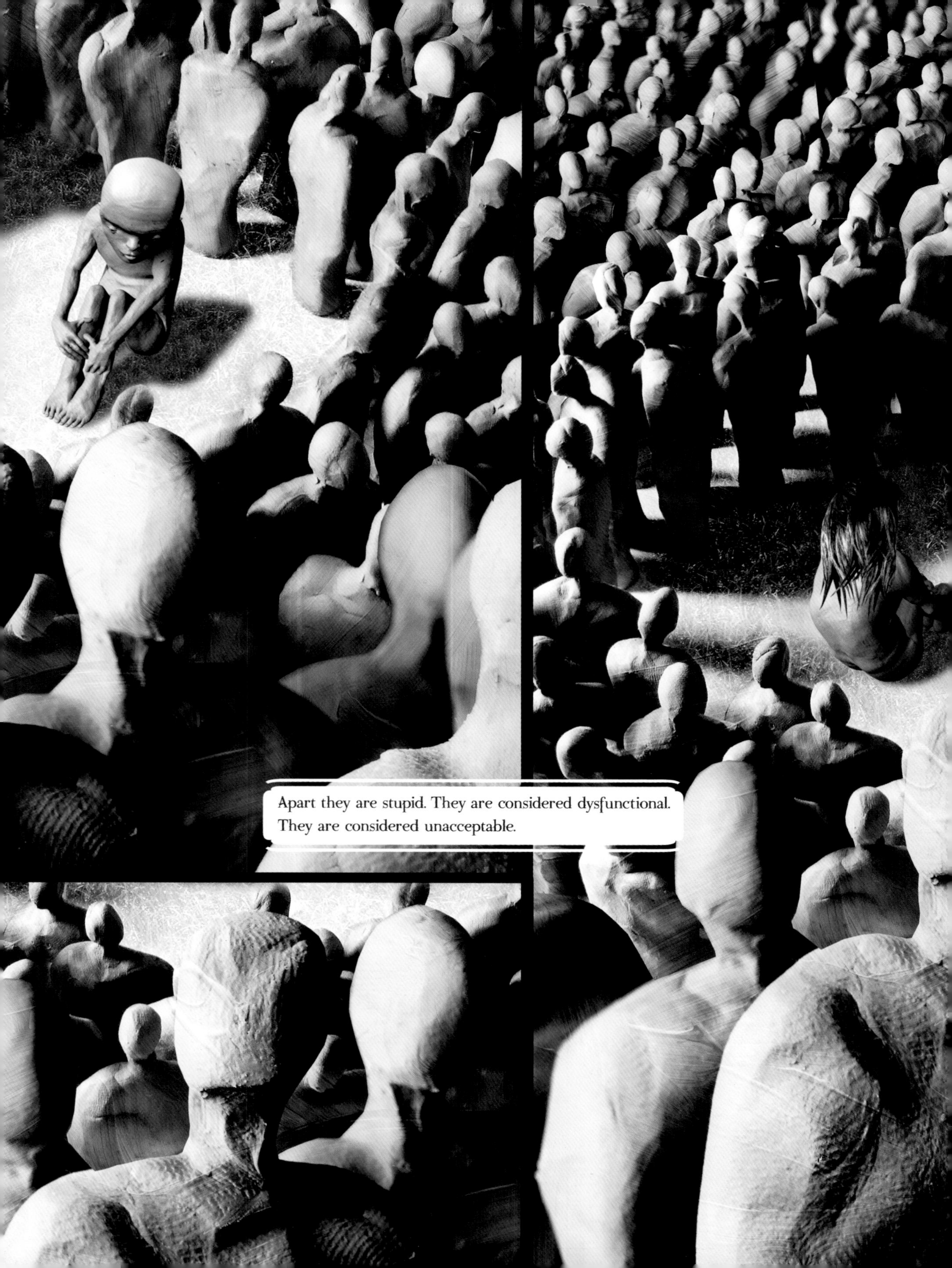
Apart they are stupid. They are considered dysfunctional. They are considered unacceptable.

On the day of application they are both drawn to the appointment.
It is in their nature to find the weak irresistible. It is the cowardice of their compulsions.
They do not think it ignoble.

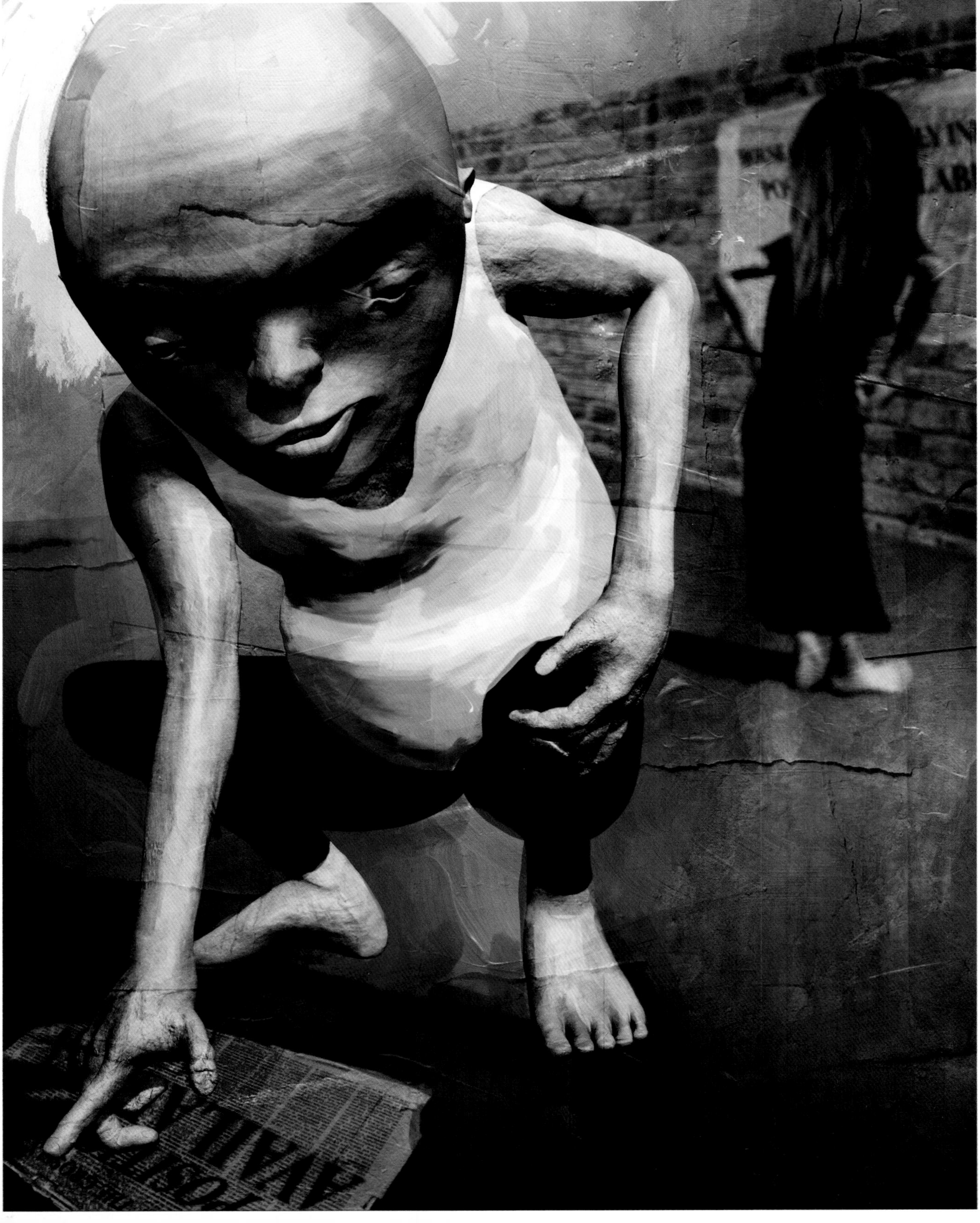

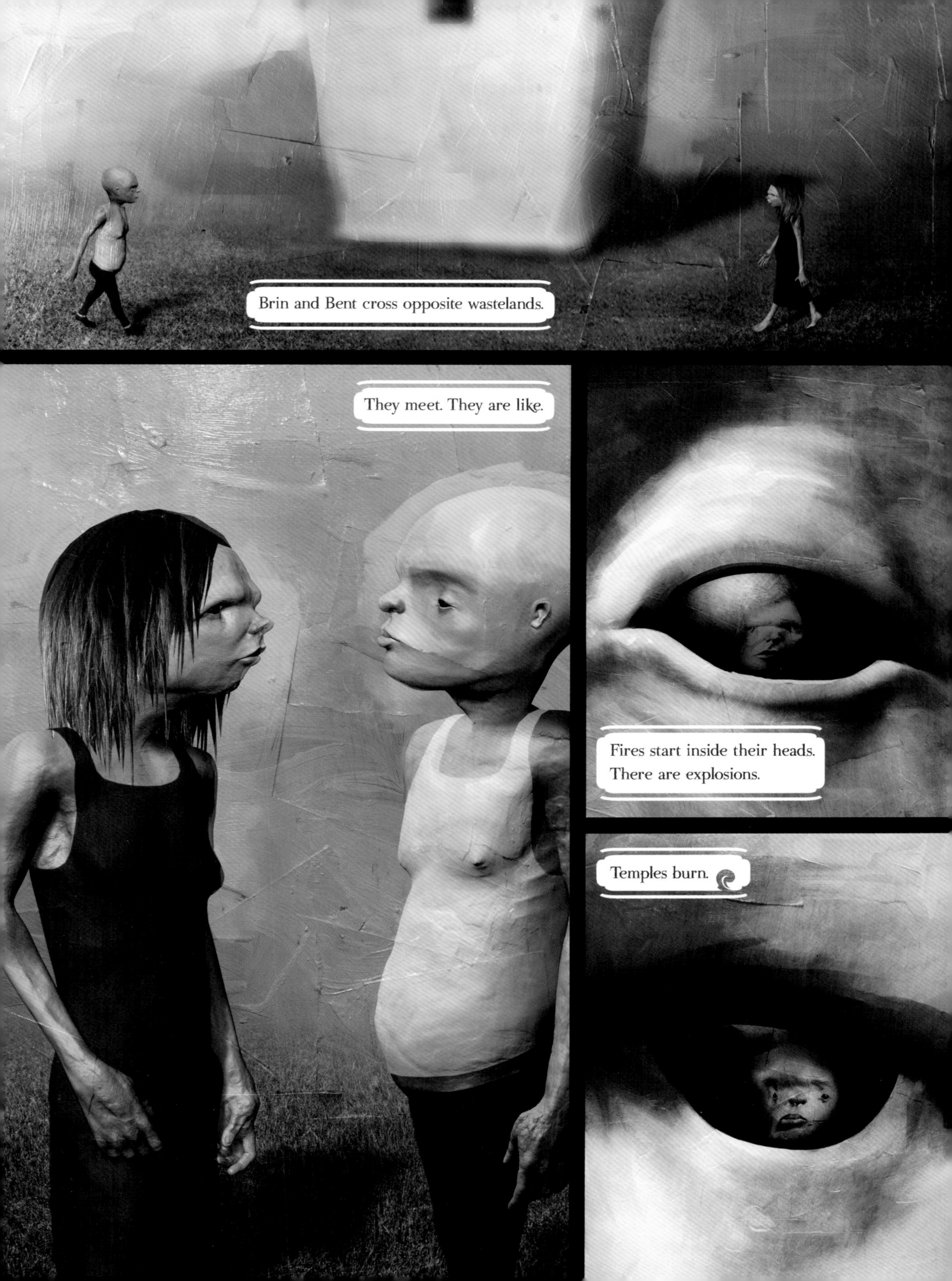
Brin and Bent cross opposite wastelands.
They meet. They are like.
Fires start inside their heads. There are explosions.
Temples burn.

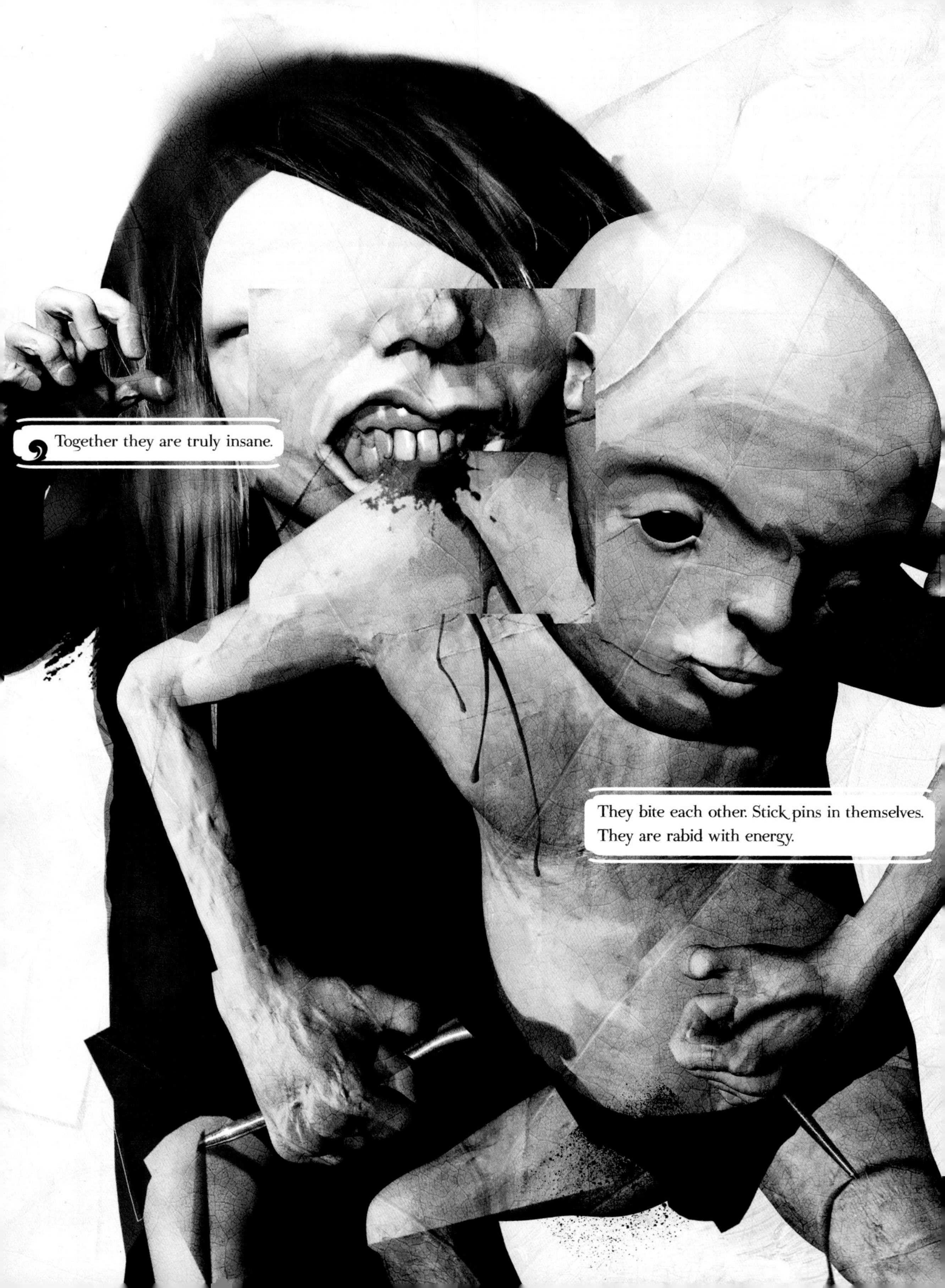
Together they are truly insane.
They bite each other. Stick pins in themselves. They are rabid with energy.

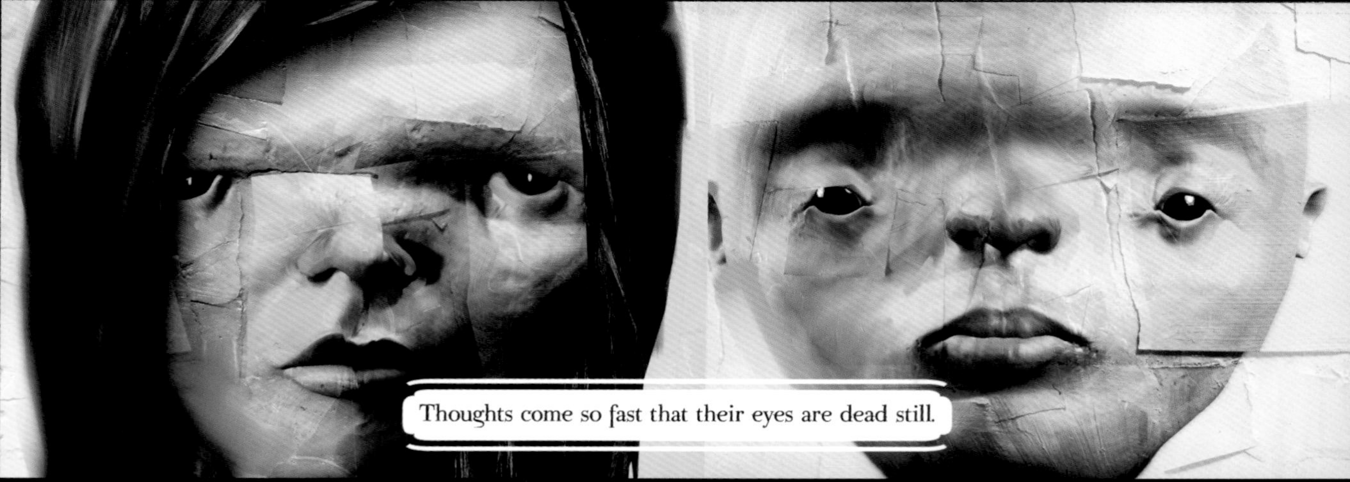
Thoughts come so fast that their eyes are dead still.

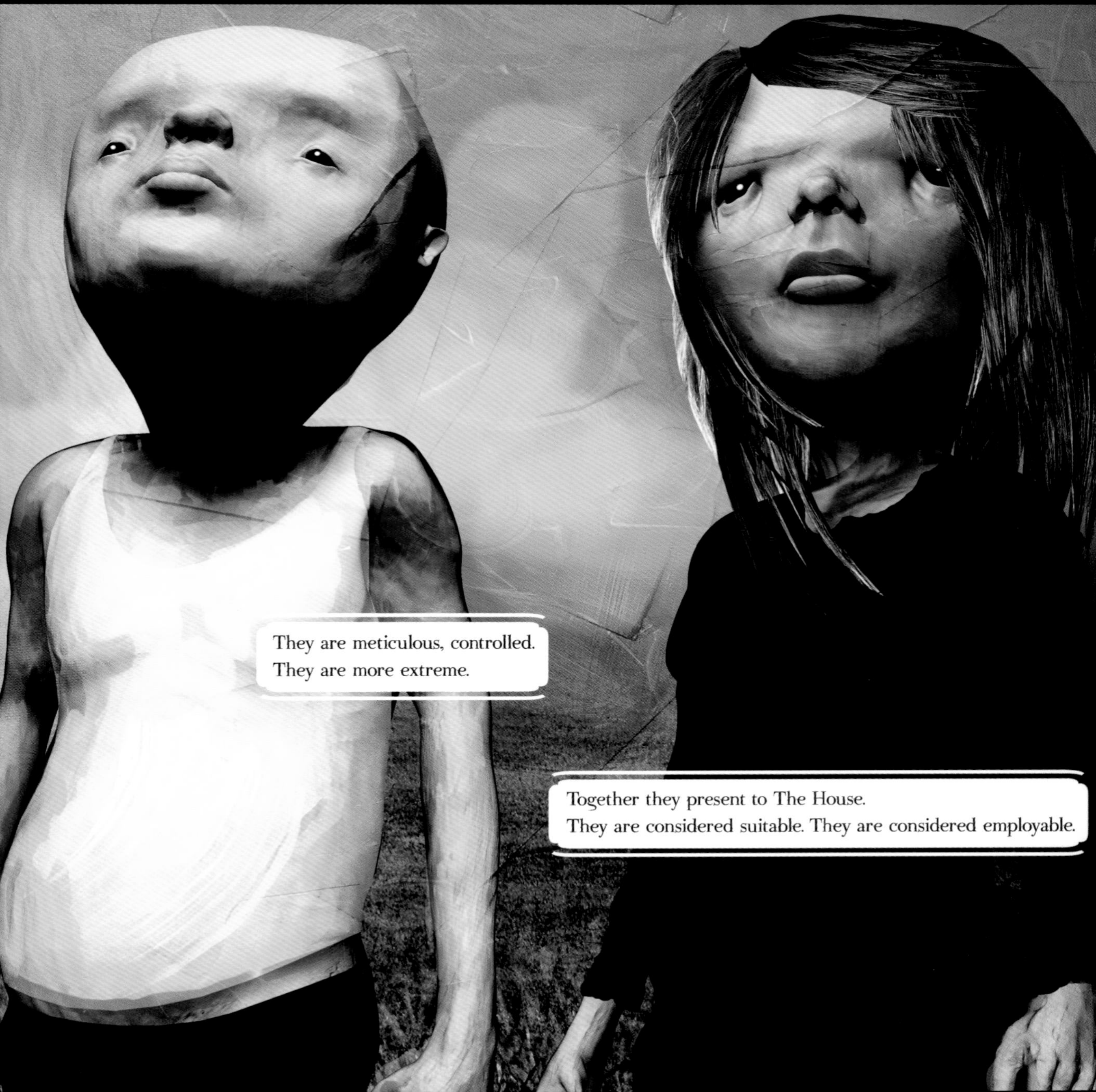
They are meticulous, controlled.
They are more extreme.
Together they present to The House.
They are considered suitable. They are considered employable.

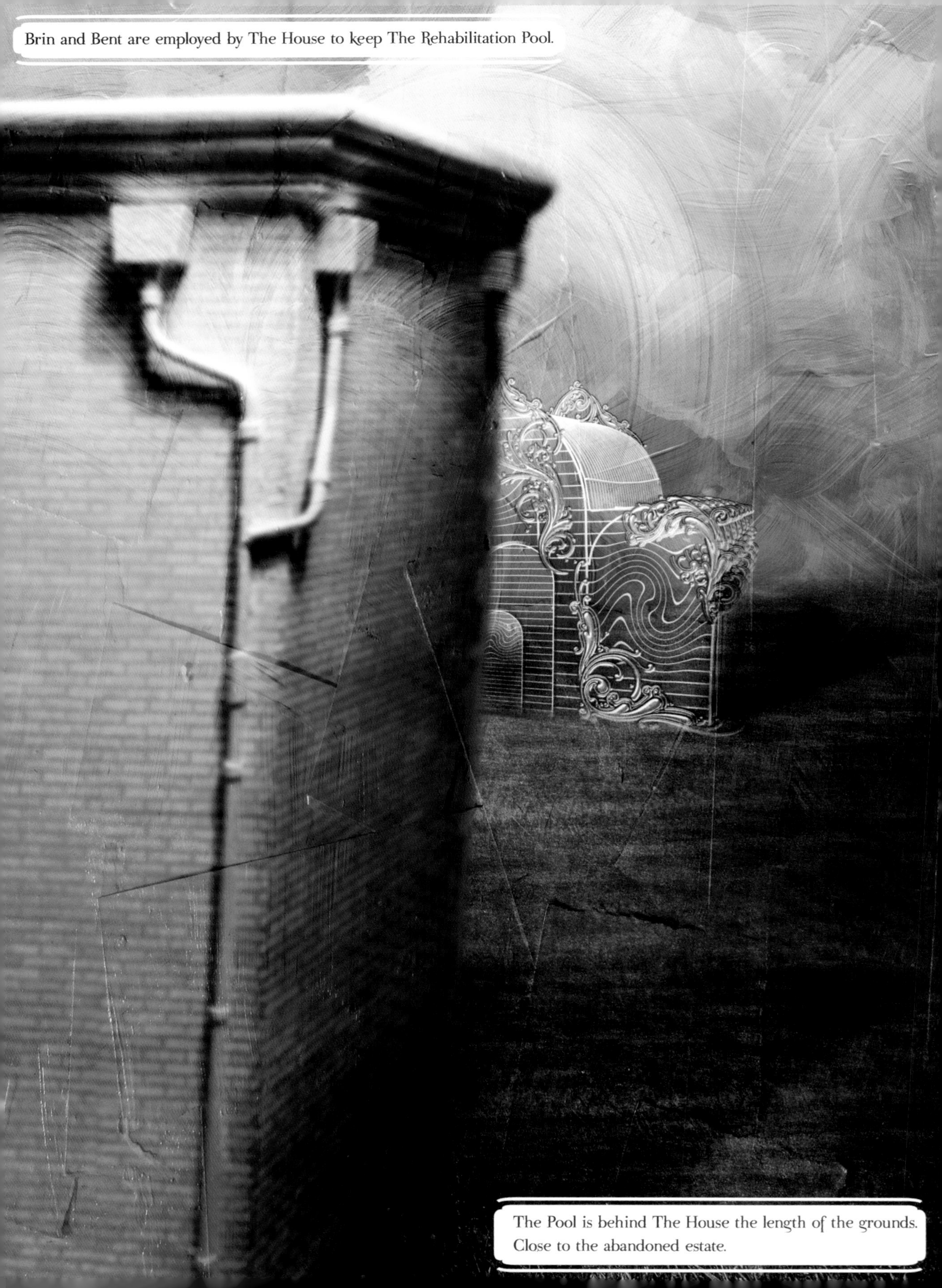
Brin and Bent are employed by The House to keep The Rehabilitation Pool.
The Pool is behind The House the length of the grounds. Close to the abandoned estate.

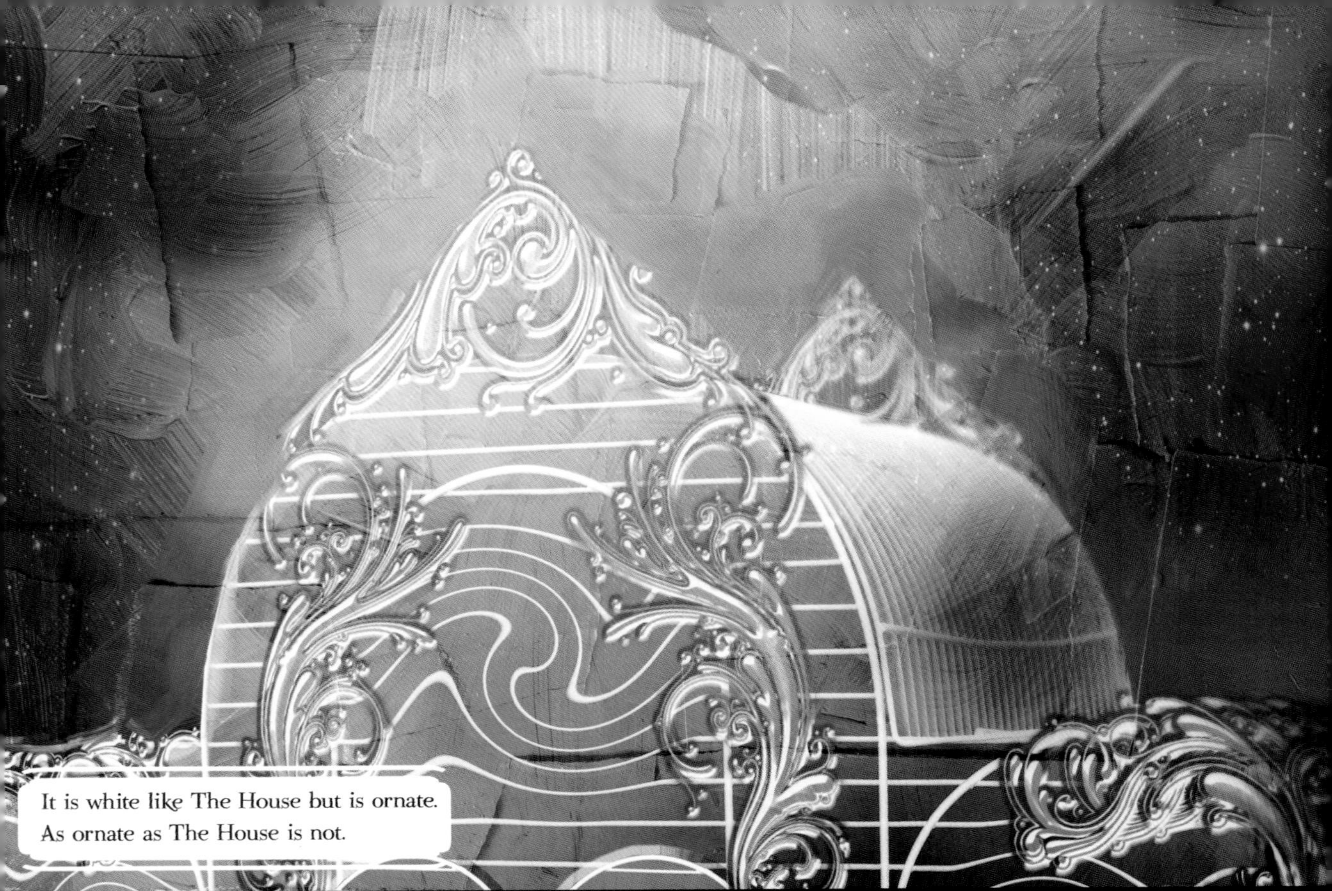
It is white like The House but is ornate.
As ornate as The House is not.

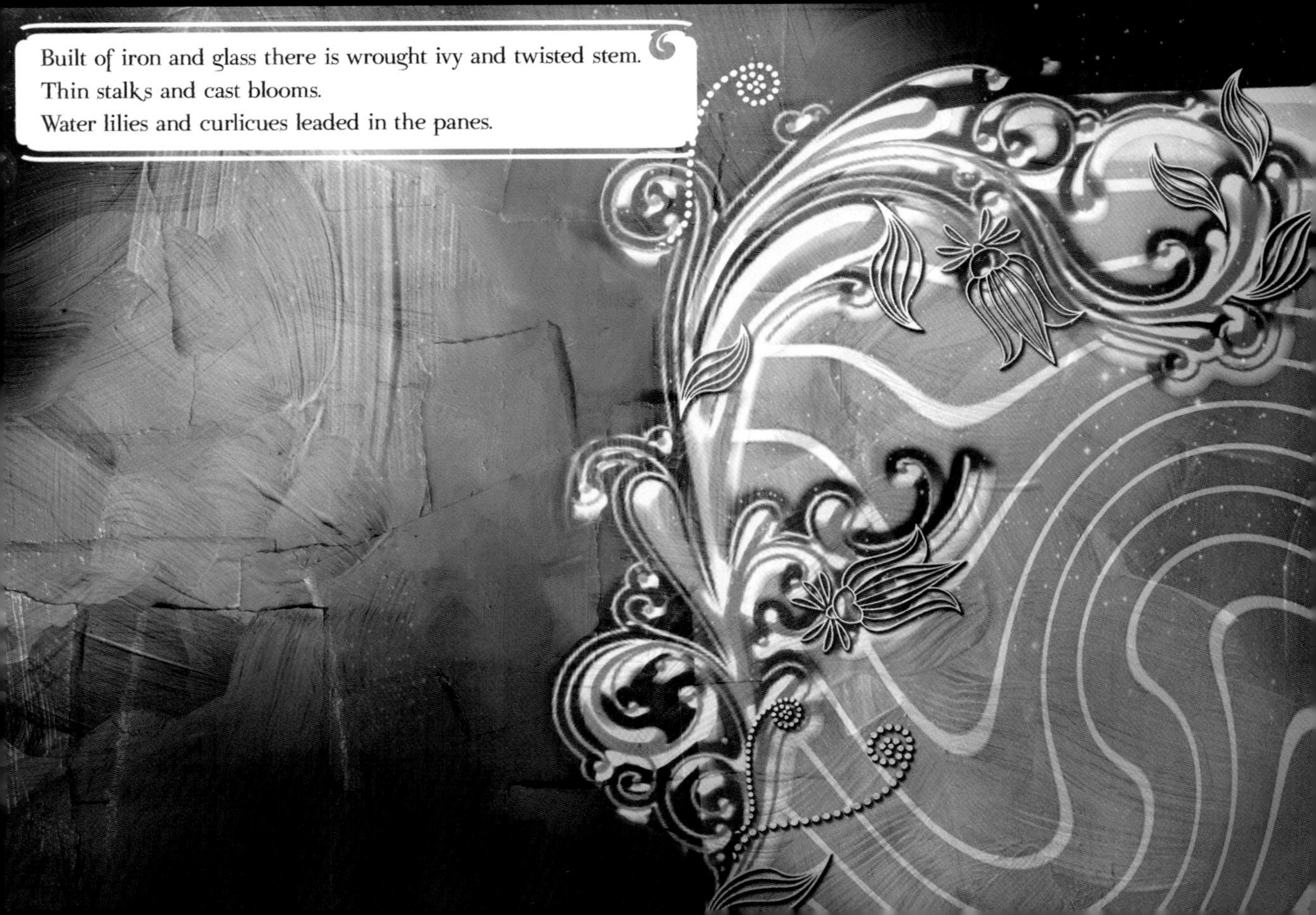
Built of iron and glass there is wrought ivy and twisted stem.
Thin stalks and cast blooms.
Water lilies and curlicues leaded in the panes.

The windows are many.
They rise, curve to the sky, dance with its light. Are pretty in the doors.

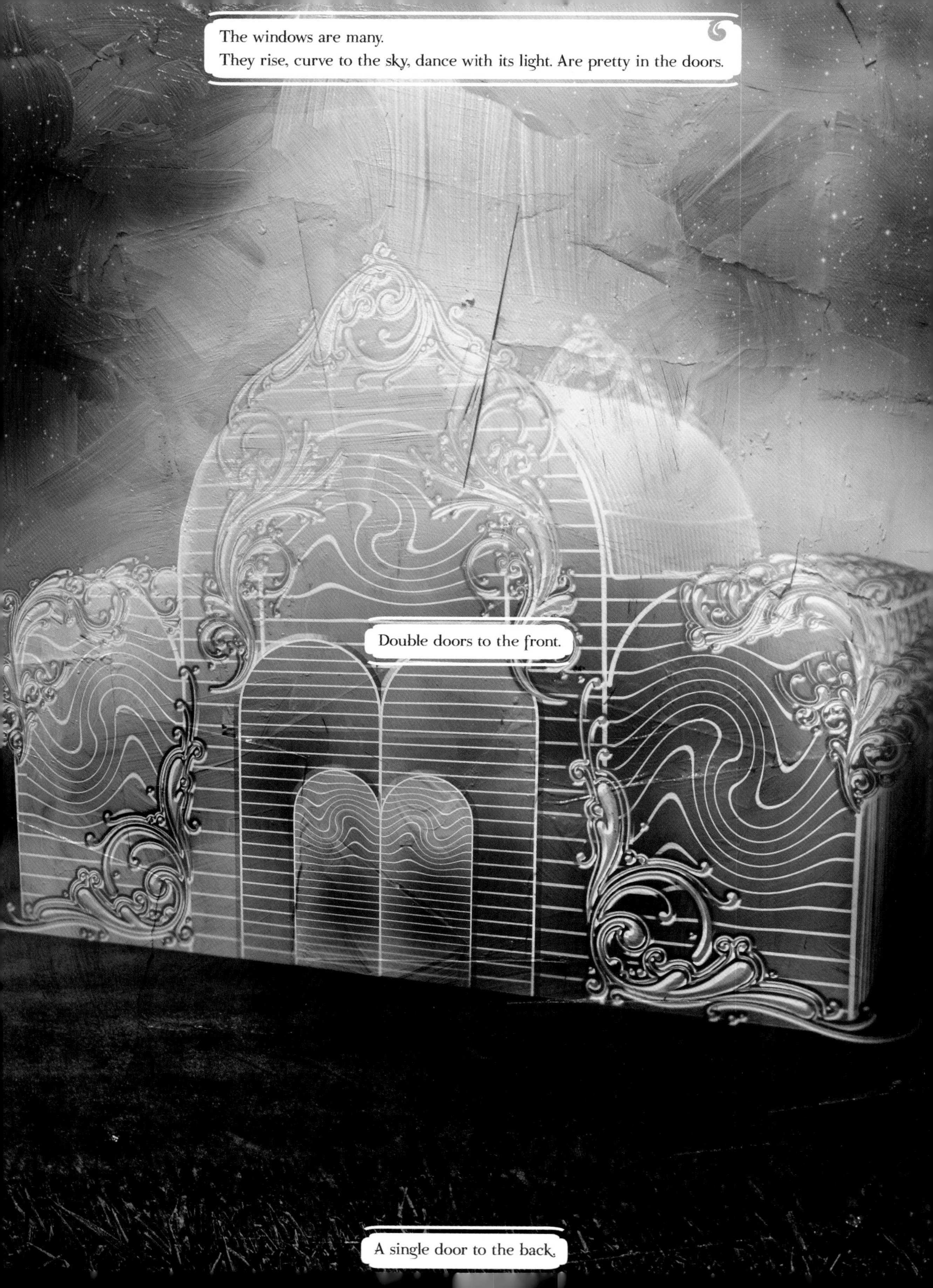

Double doors to the front.

A single door to the back.

The back door is locked. There is no key.

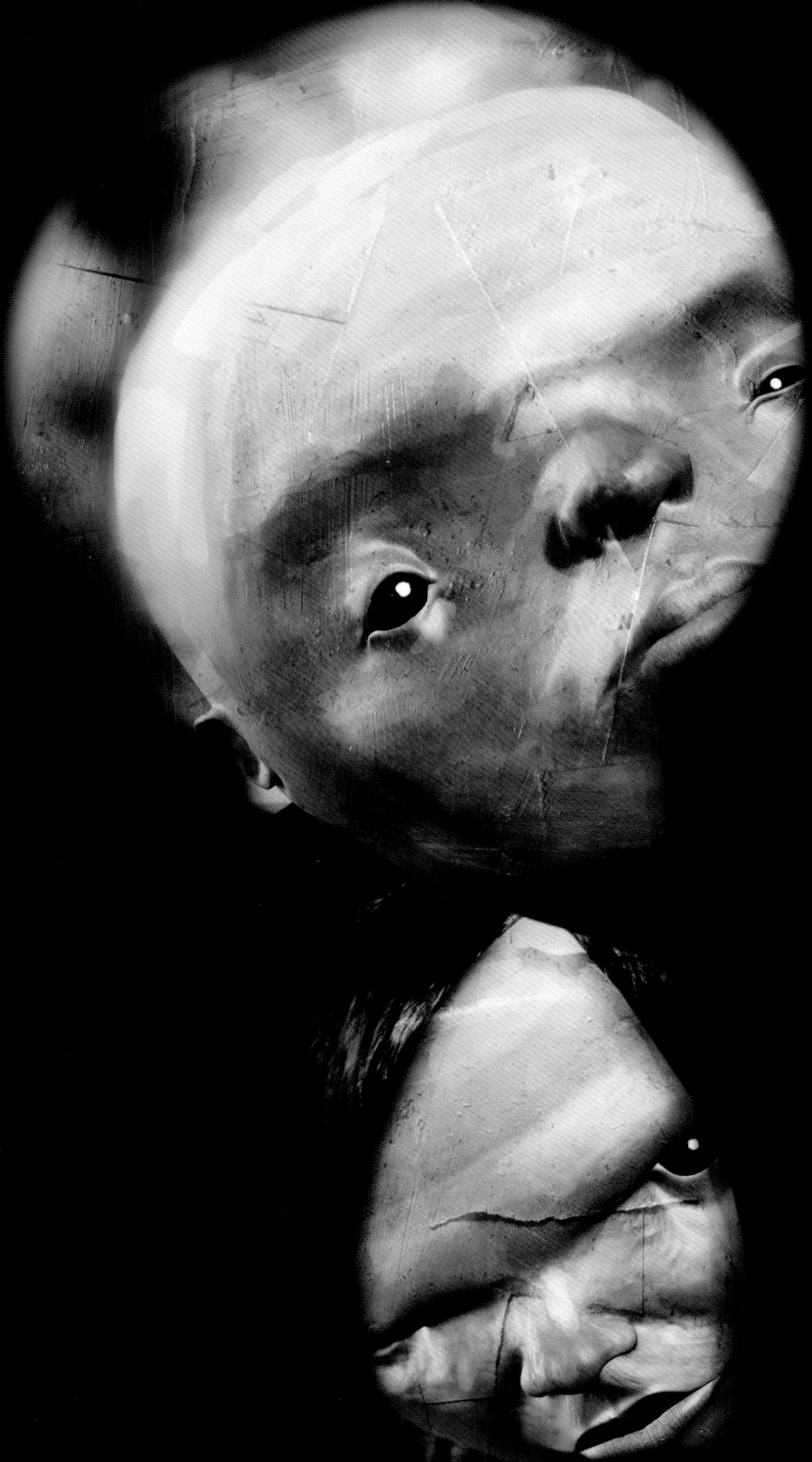

There has been no key to the back door of The Pool for as long as The House can recall.

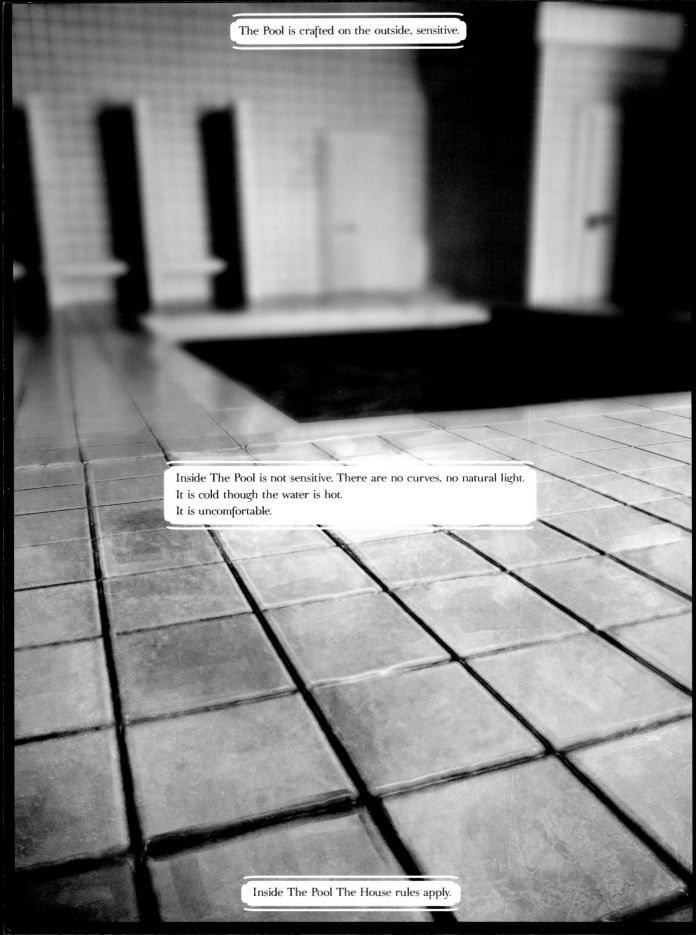

The Pool is crafted on the outside, sensitive.

Inside The Pool is not sensitive. There are no curves, no natural light.
It is cold though the water is hot.
It is uncomfortable.

Inside The Pool The House rules apply.

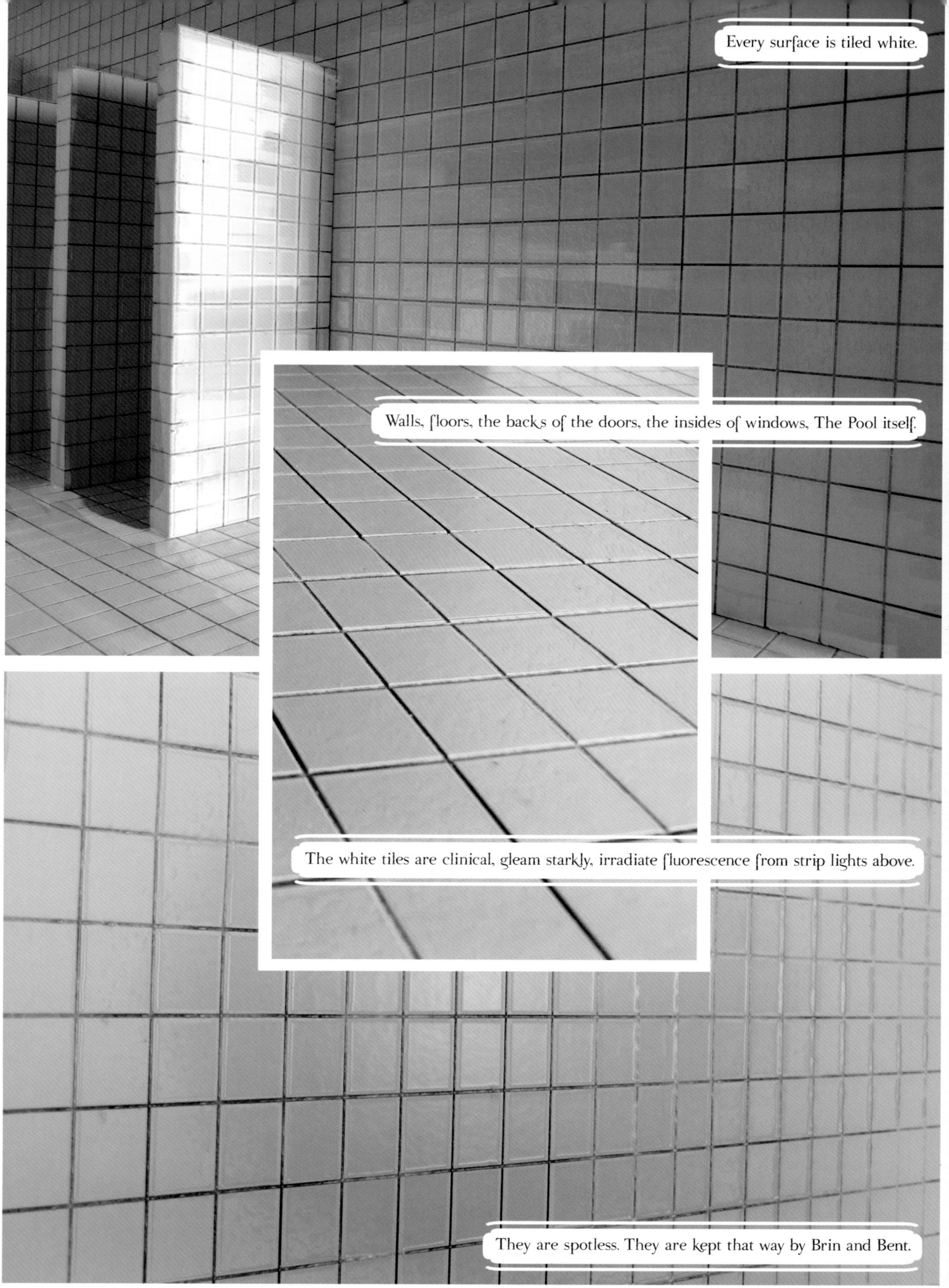
Every surface is tiled white.
Walls, floors, the backs of the doors, the insides of windows, The Pool itself.
The white tiles are clinical, gleam starkly, irradiate fluorescence from strip lights above.
They are spotless. They are kept that way by Brin and Bent.

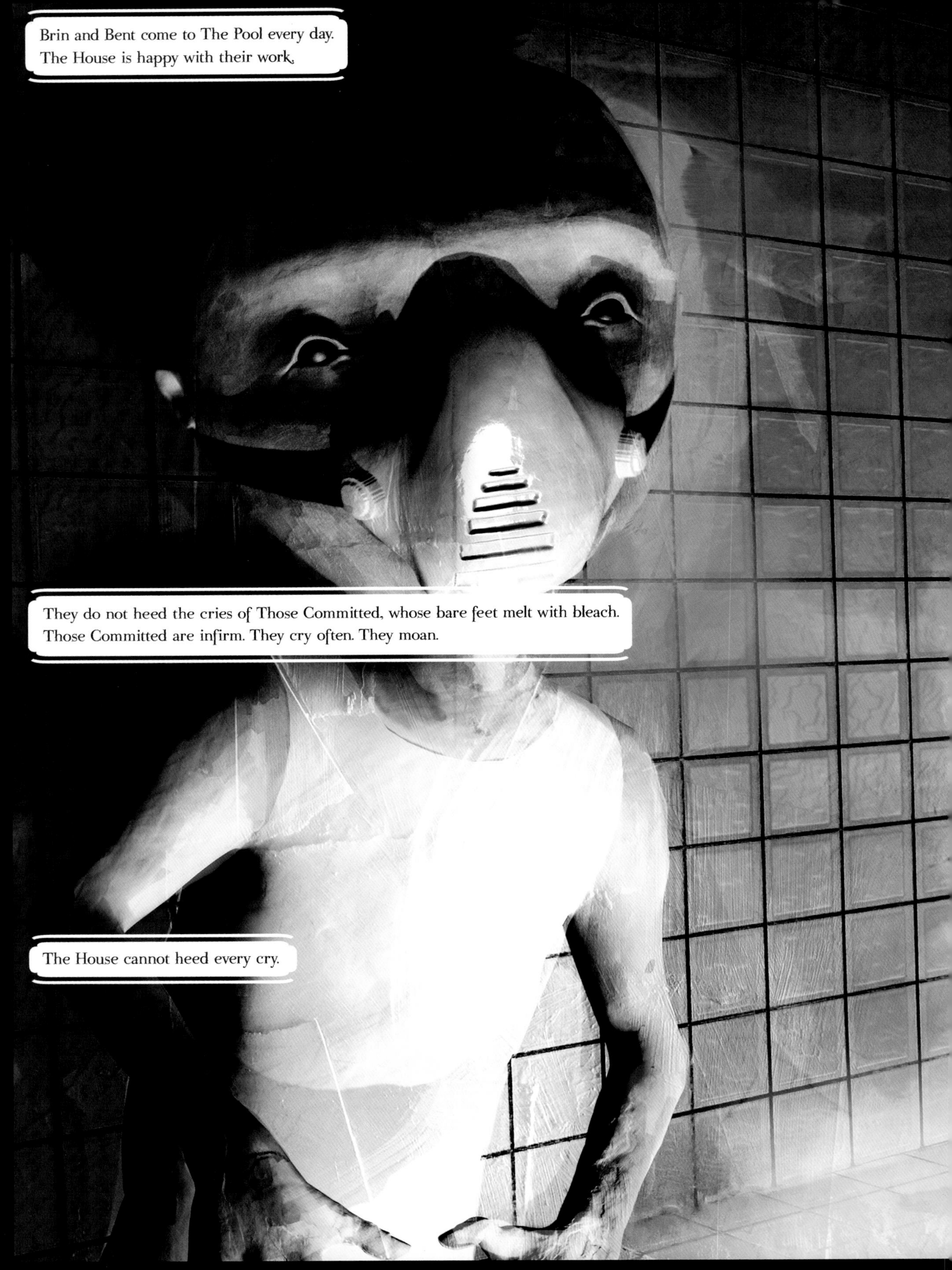
Brin and Bent come to The Pool every day.
The House is happy with their work.
They do not heed the cries of Those Committed, whose bare feet melt with bleach.
Those Committed are infirm. They cry often. They moan.
The House cannot heed every cry.

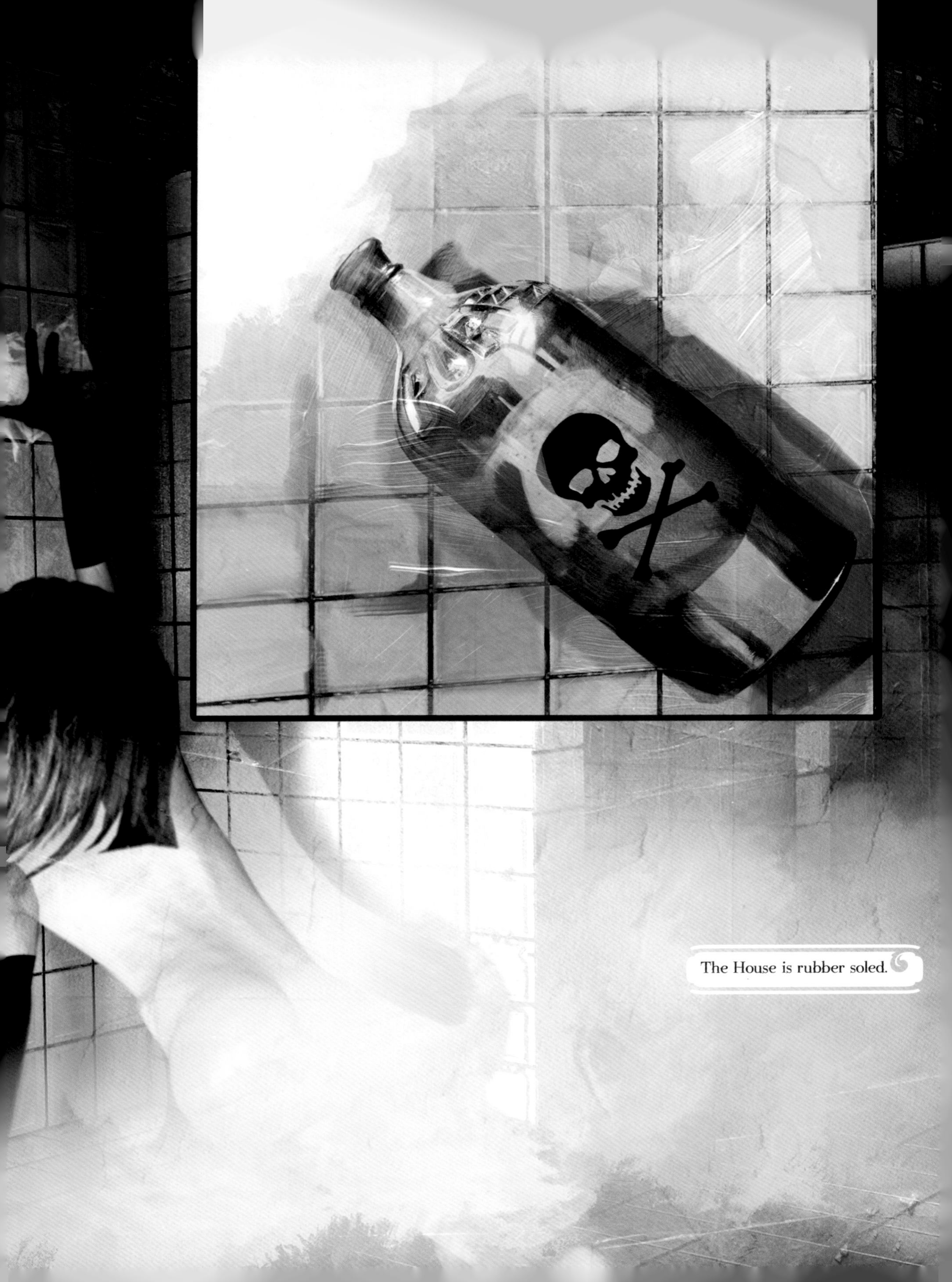

The House is rubber soled.

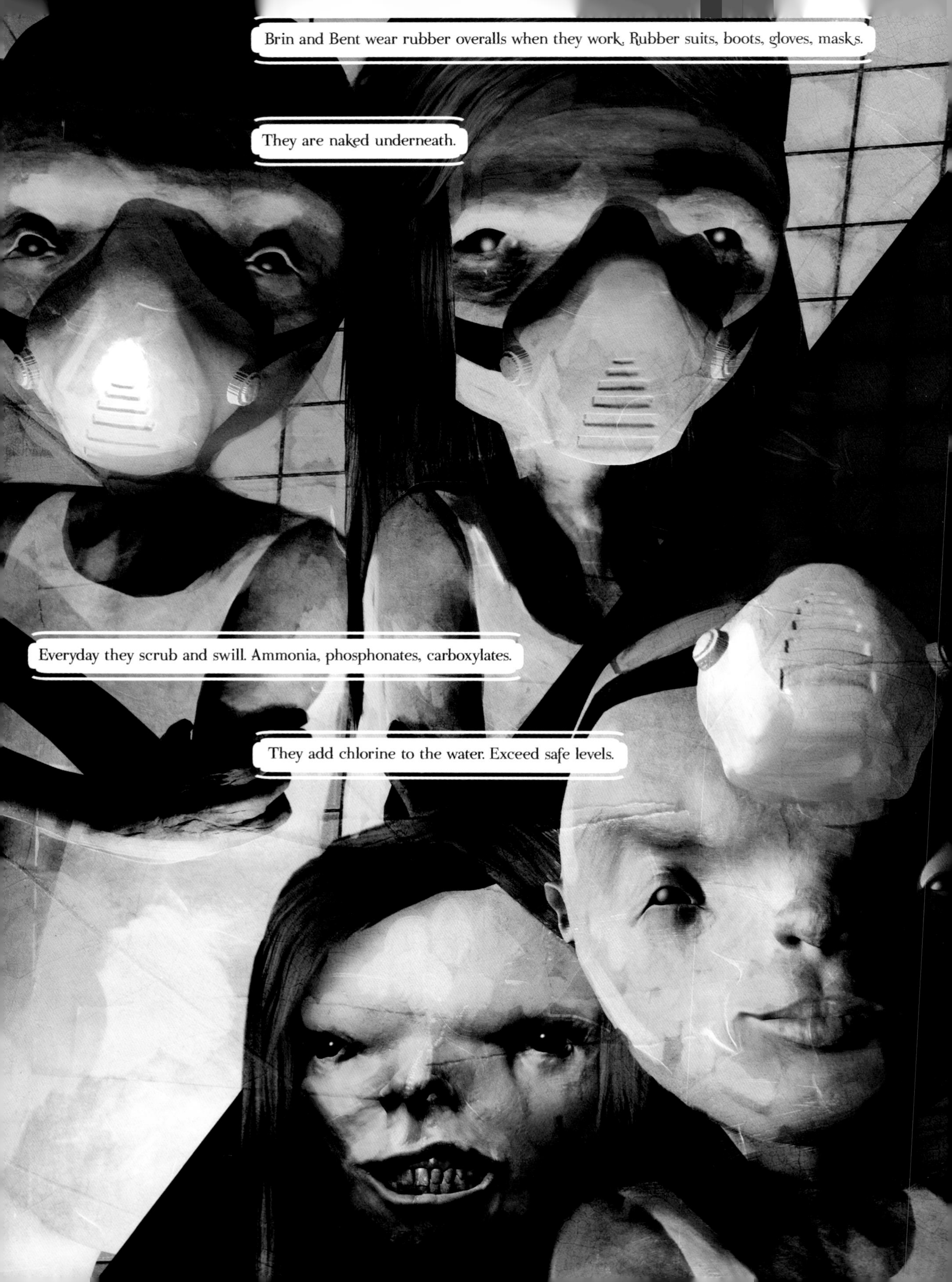
Brin and Bent wear rubber overalls when they work. Rubber suits, boots, gloves, masks.
They are naked underneath.
Everyday they scrub and swill. Ammonia, phosphonates, carboxylates.
They add chlorine to the water. Exceed safe levels.

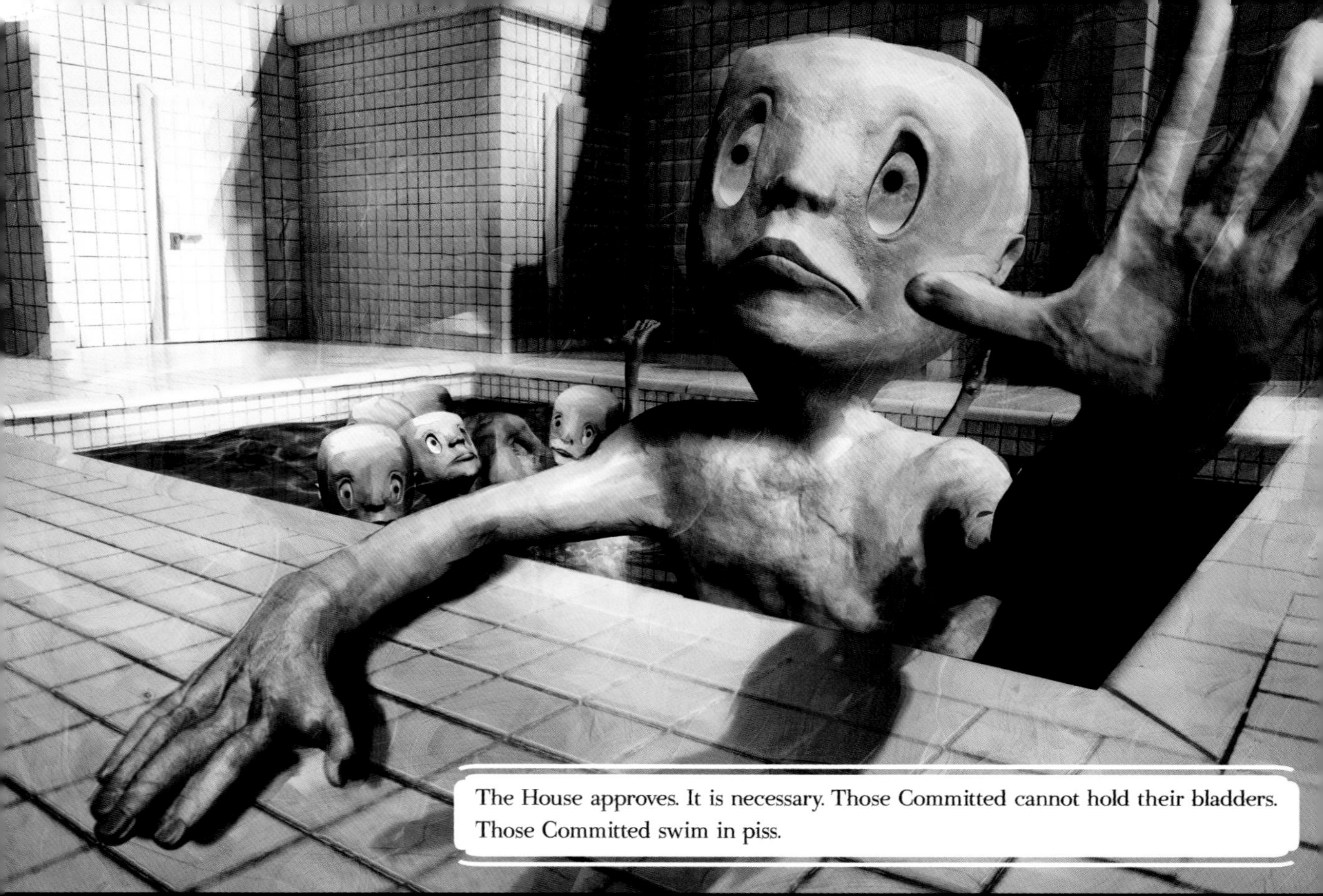
The House approves. It is necessary. Those Committed cannot hold their bladders. Those Committed swim in piss.

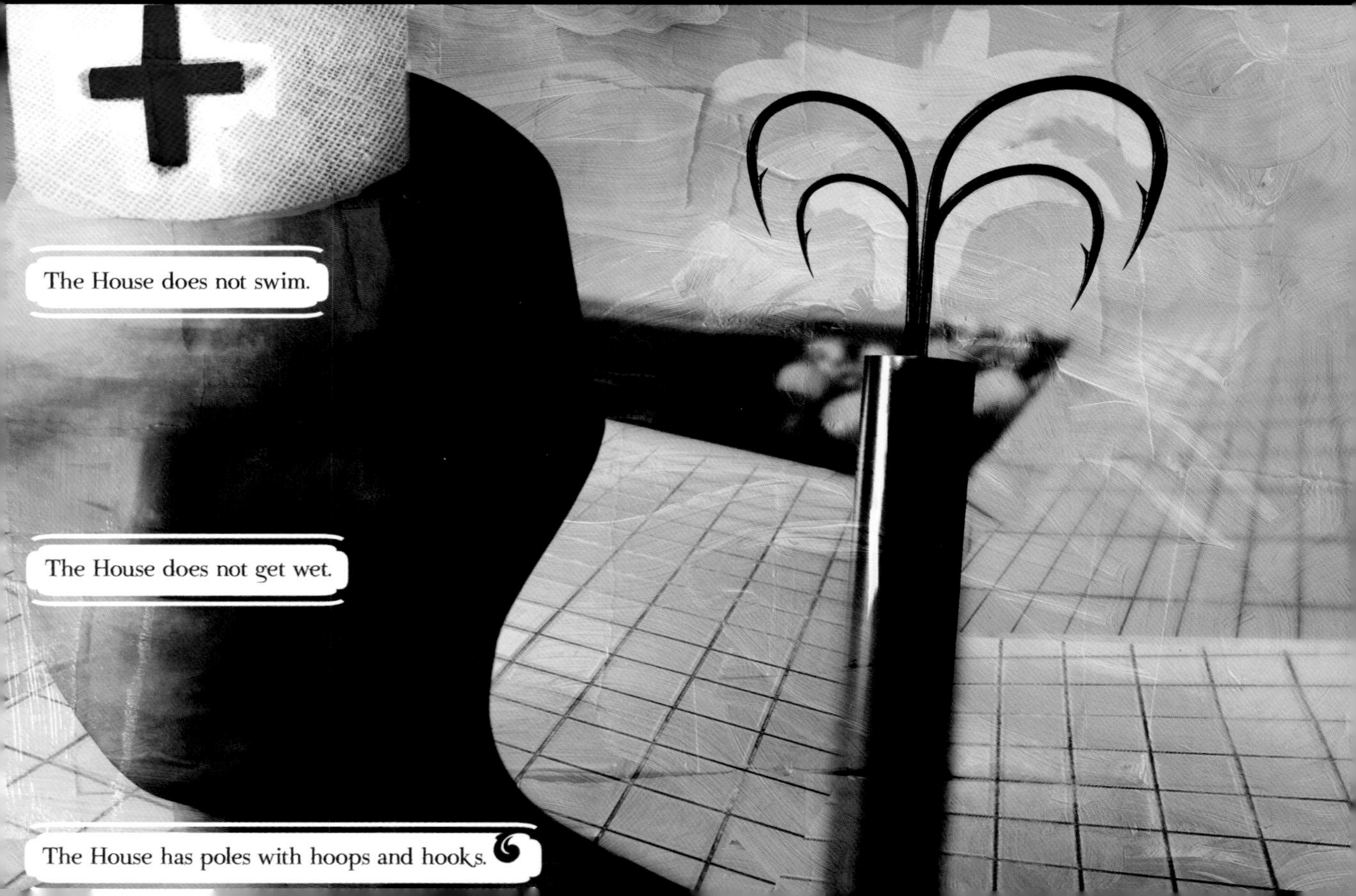
The House does not swim.
The House does not get wet.
The House has poles with hoops and hooks.

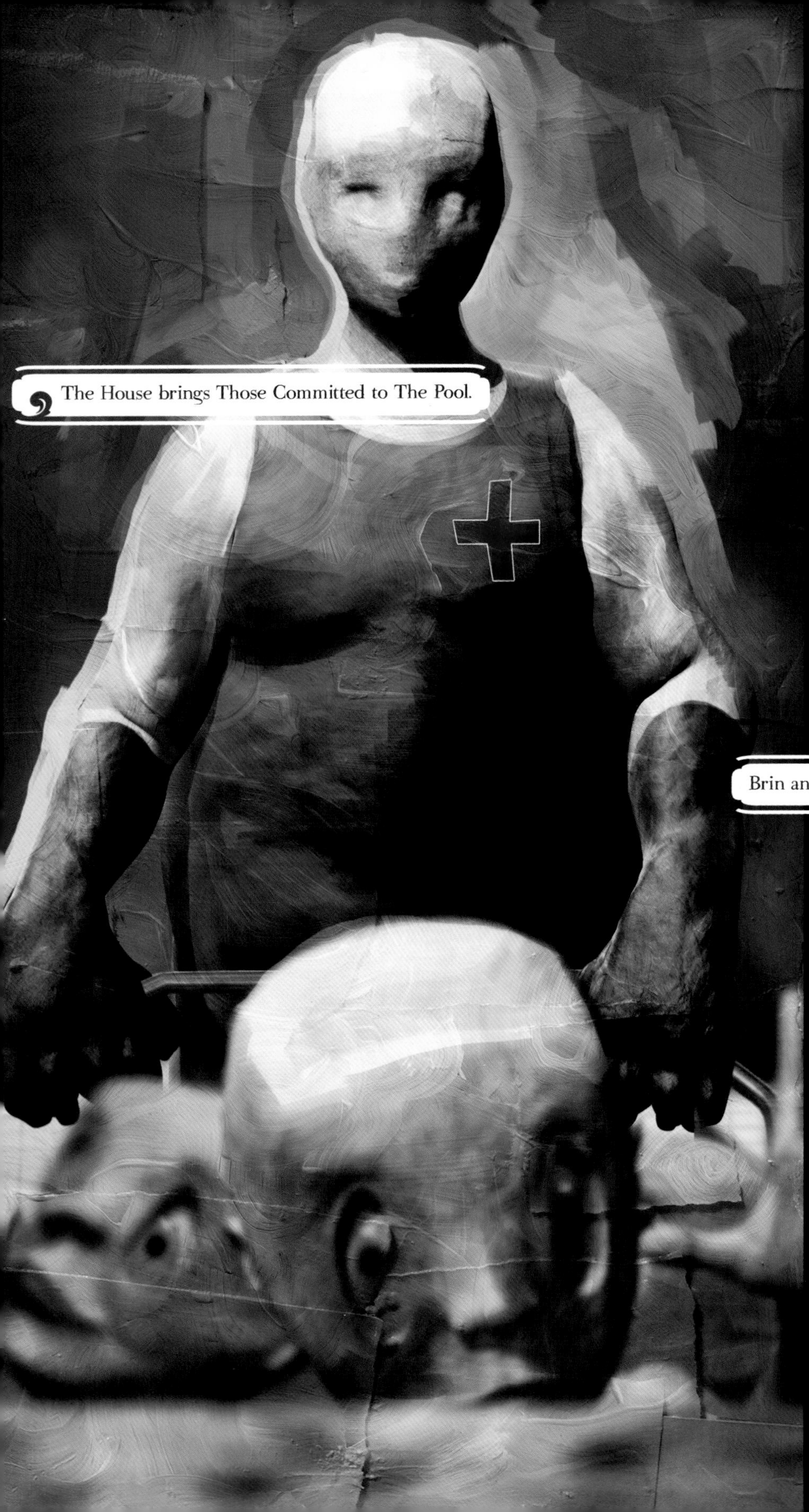
The House brings Those Committed to The Pool.
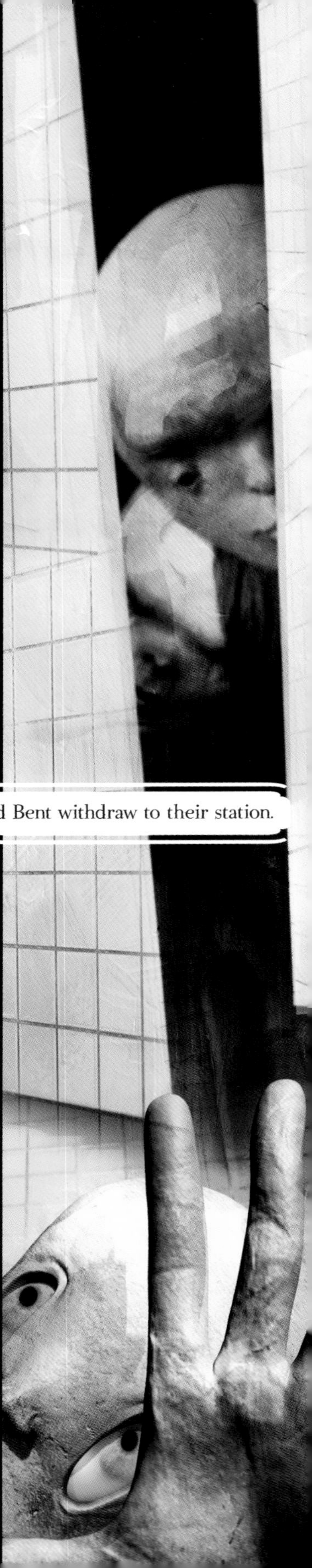
Brin and Bent withdraw to their station.

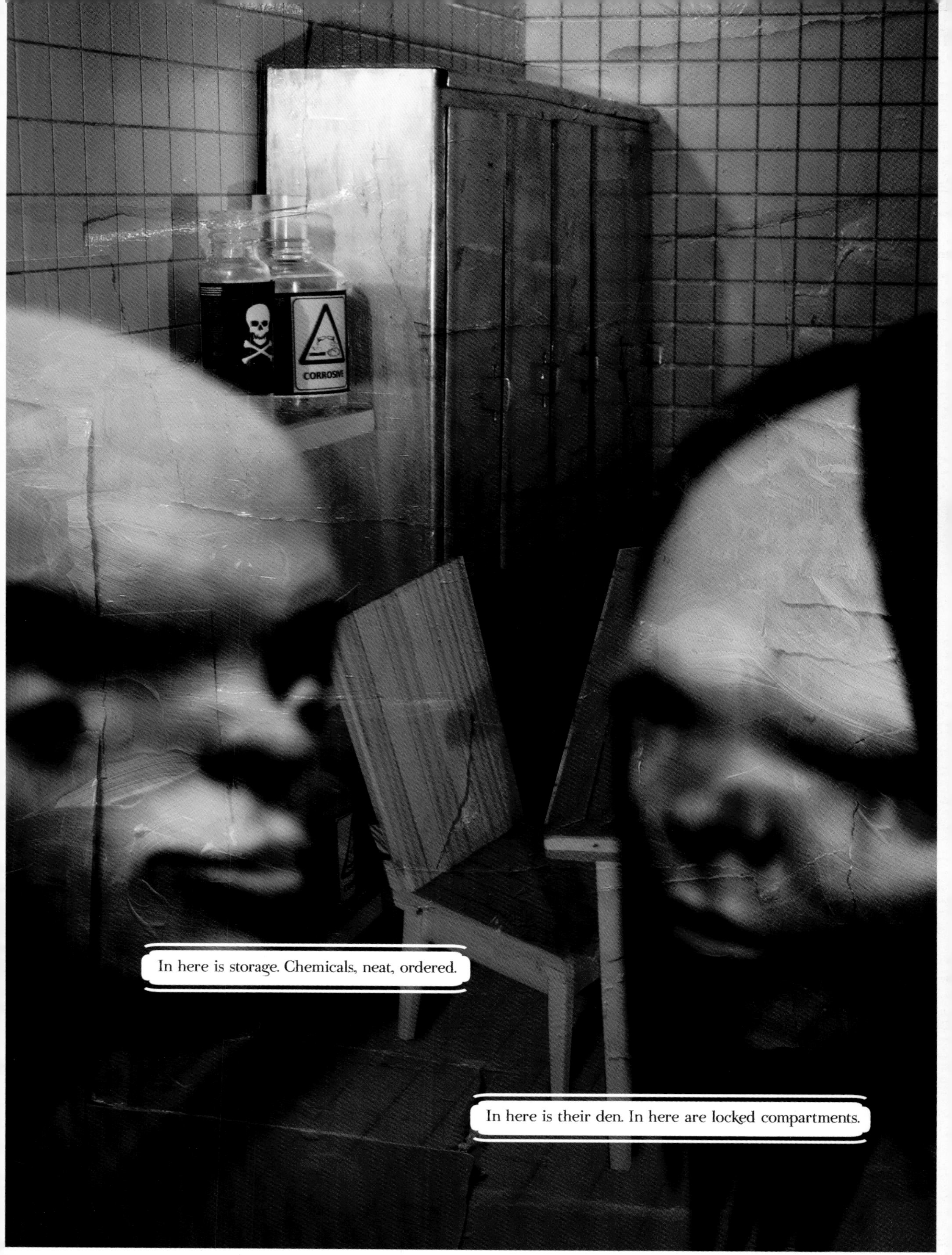
CORROSIVE
In here is storage. Chemicals, neat, ordered.
In here is their den. In here are locked compartments.

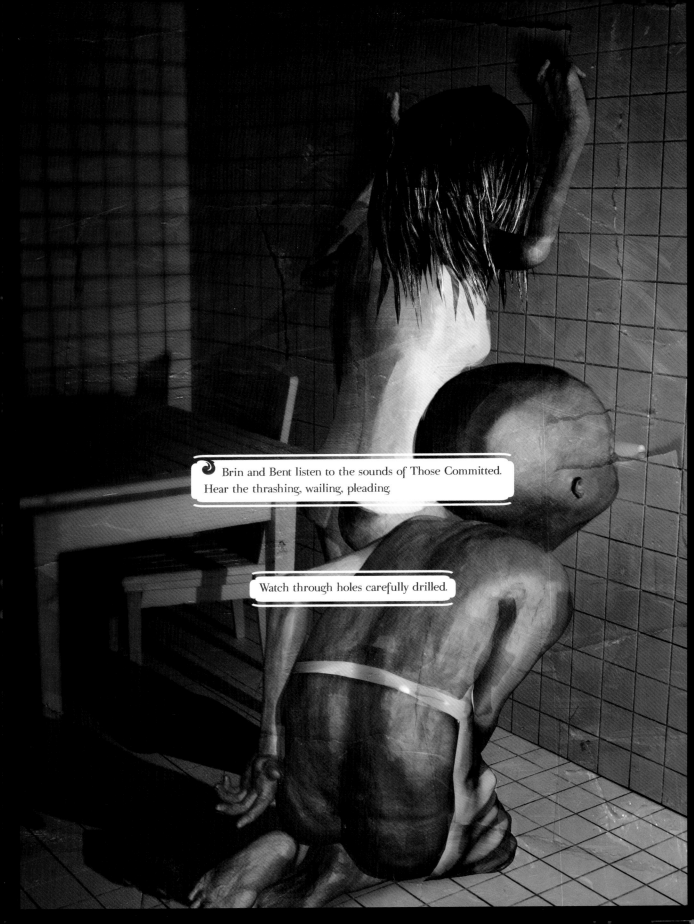

Brin and Bent listen to the sounds of Those Committed. Hear the thrashing, wailing, pleading.

Watch through holes carefully drilled.

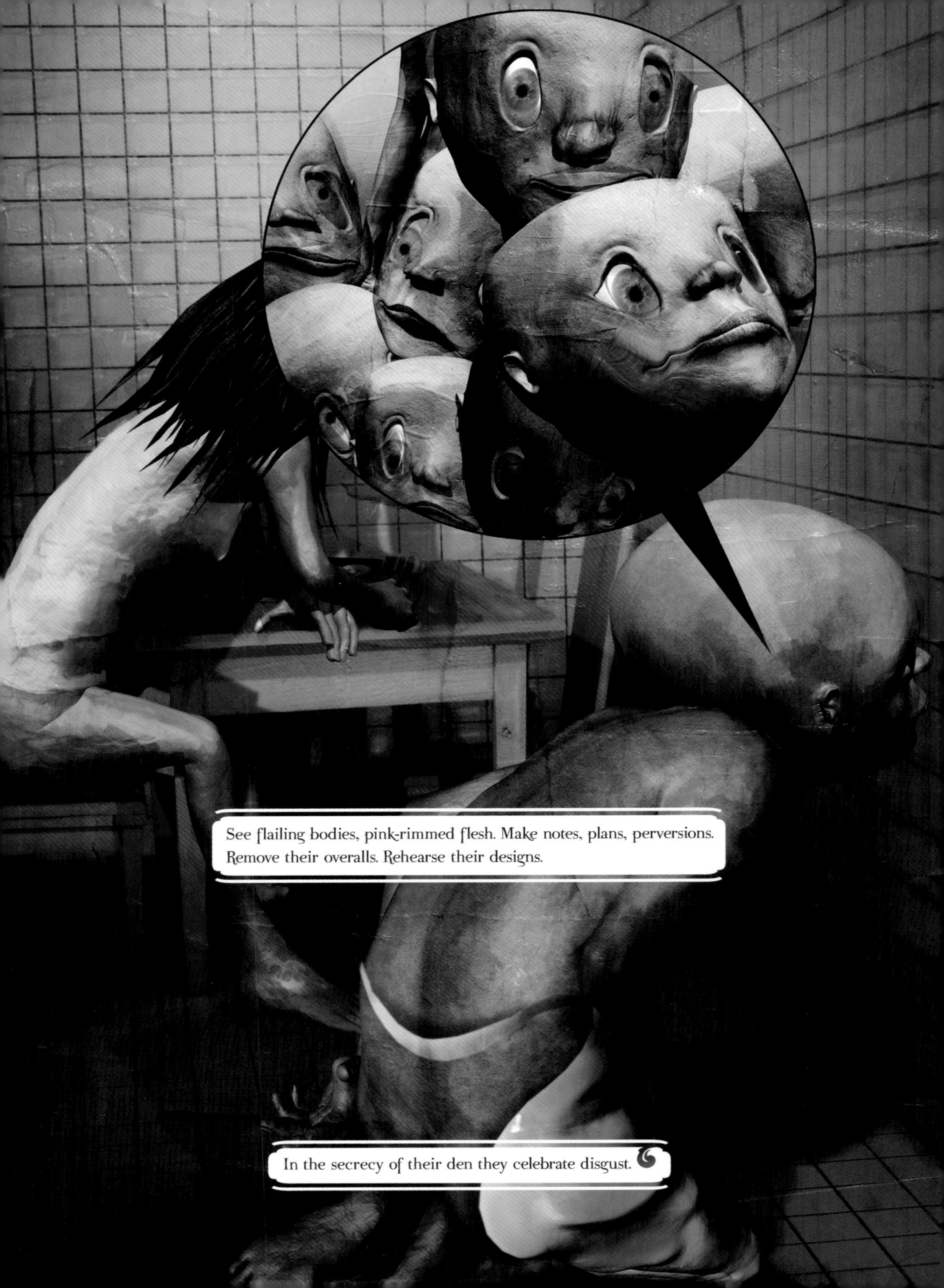
See flailing bodies, pink-rimmed flesh. Make notes, plans, perversions. Remove their overalls. Rehearse their designs.
In the secrecy of their den they celebrate disgust.

Their language is physical. Hard beating, hard sex. It is how they communicate. They do not speak.
Together their silence is complicit. Defining their own consciences.

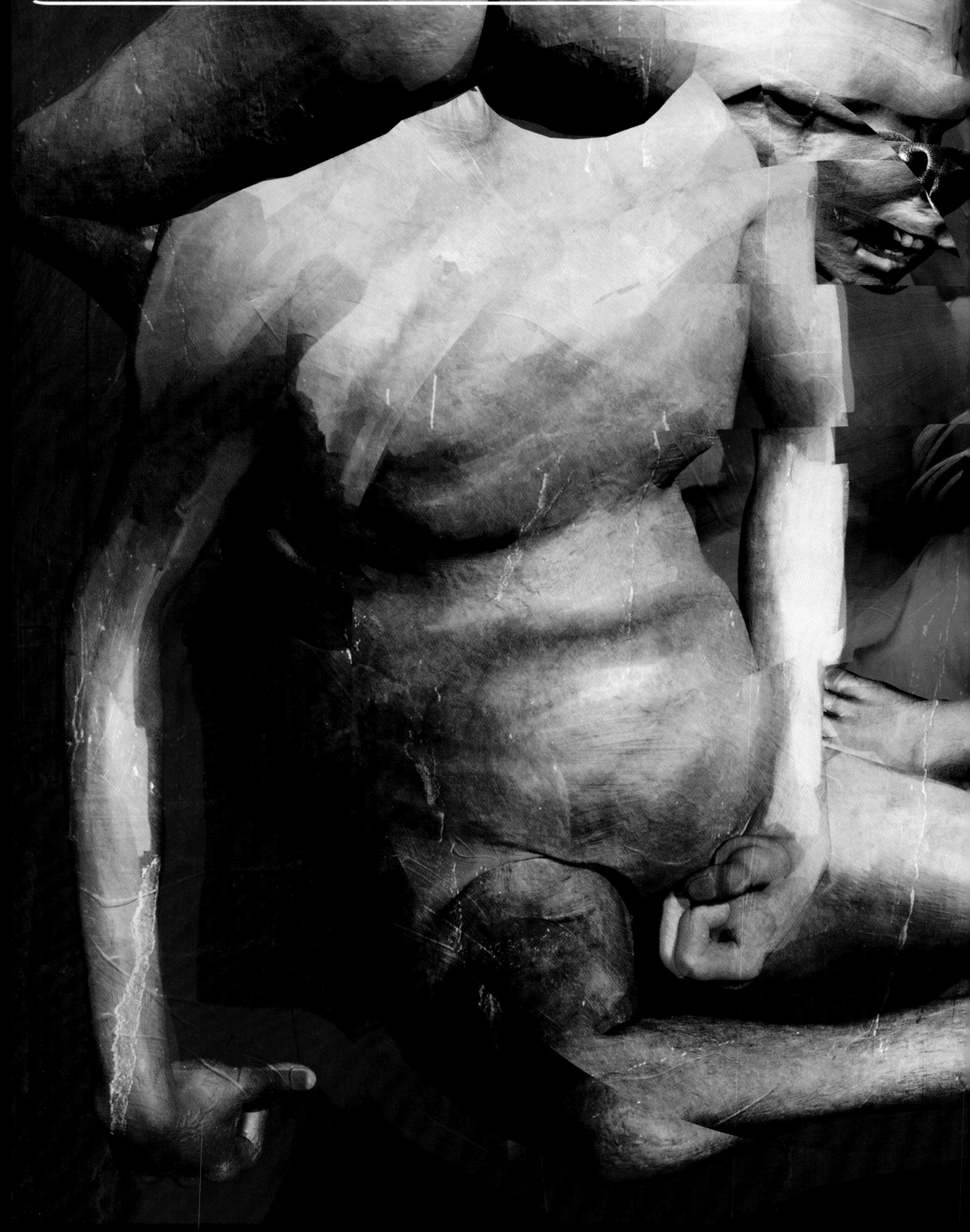

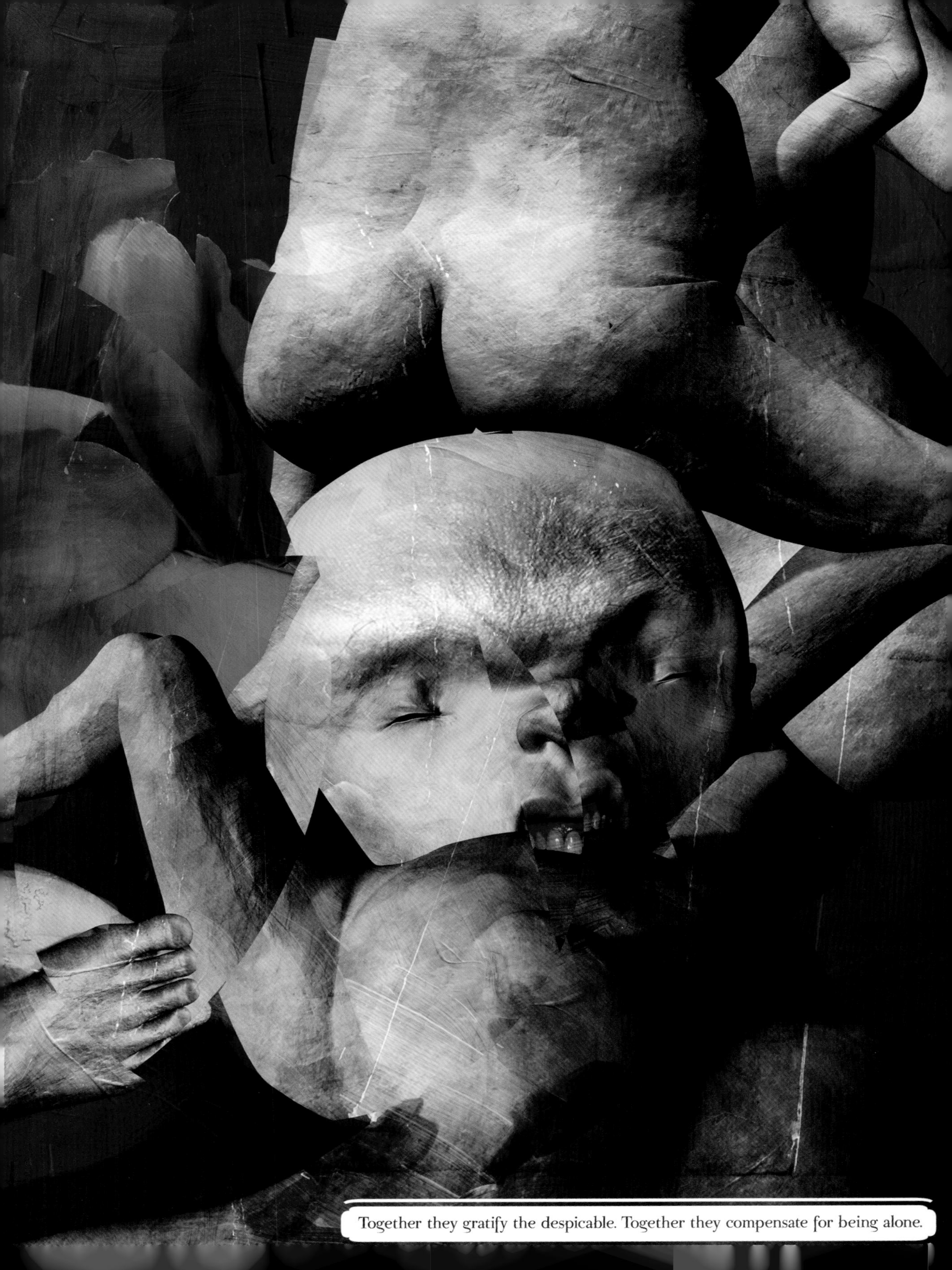

Together they gratify the despicable. Together they compensate for being alone.

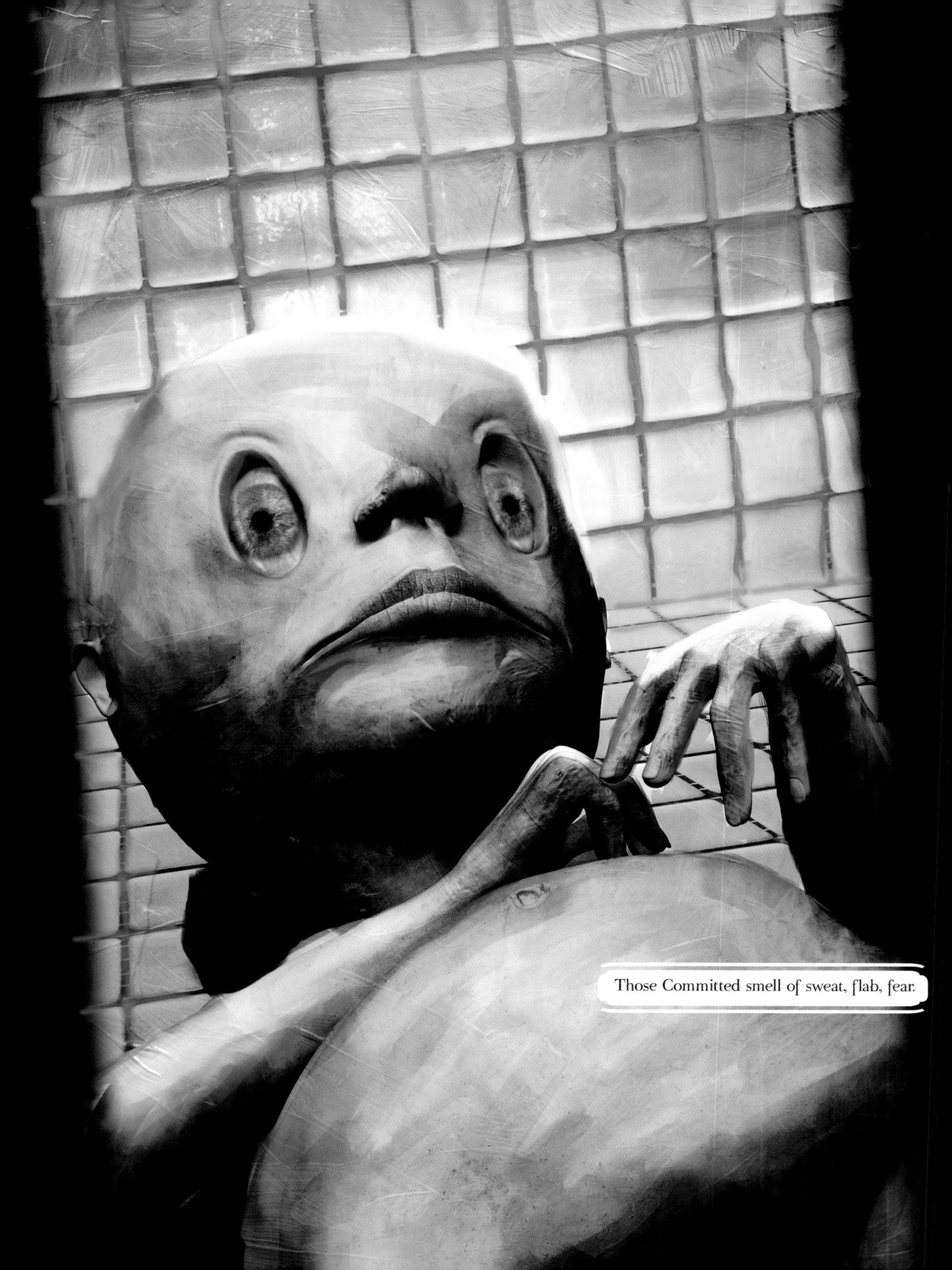

Those Committed smell of sweat, flab, fear.

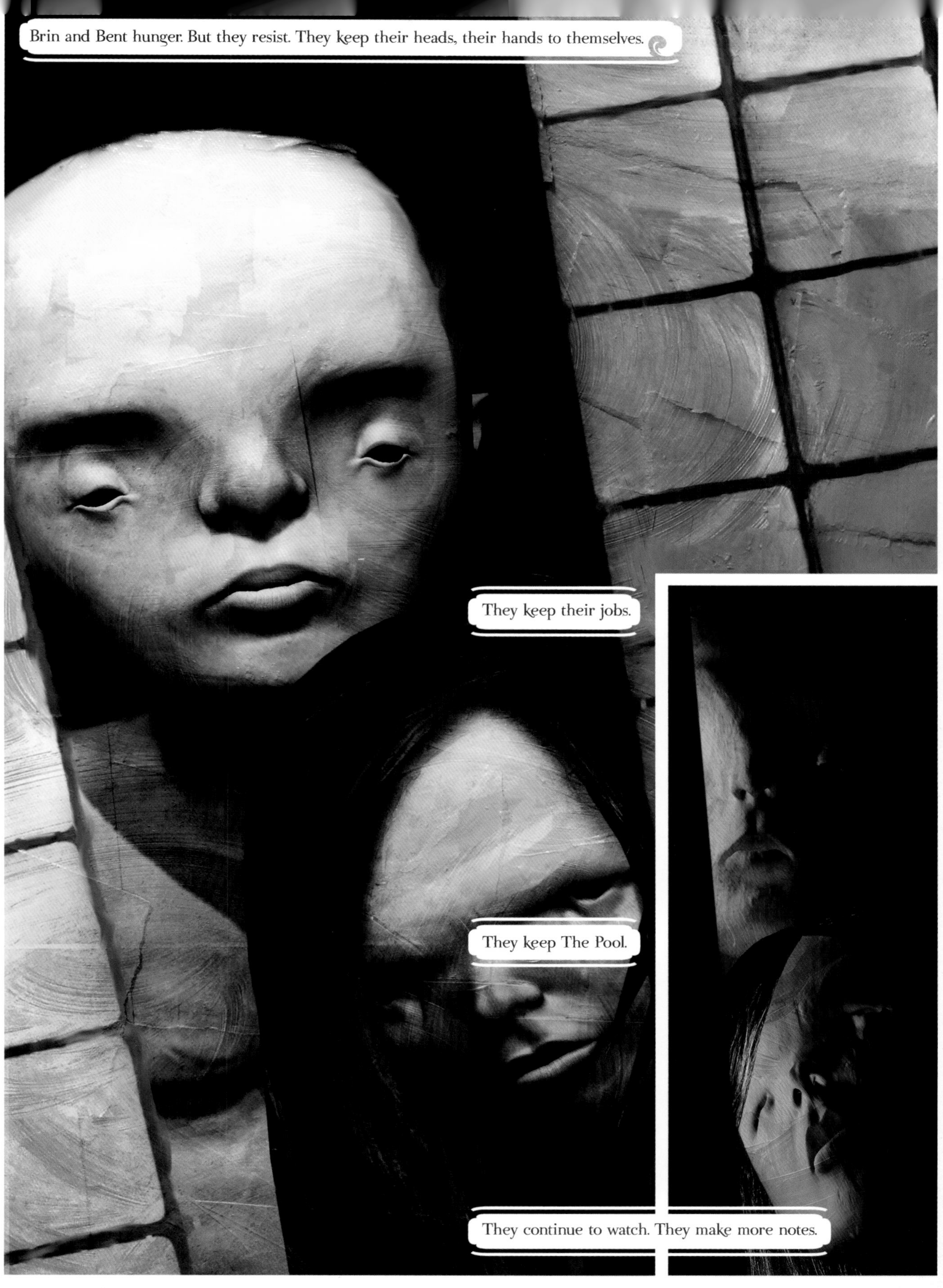
Brin and Bent hunger. But they resist. They keep their heads, their hands to themselves.
They keep their jobs.
They keep The Pool.
They continue to watch. They make more notes.

PART 2

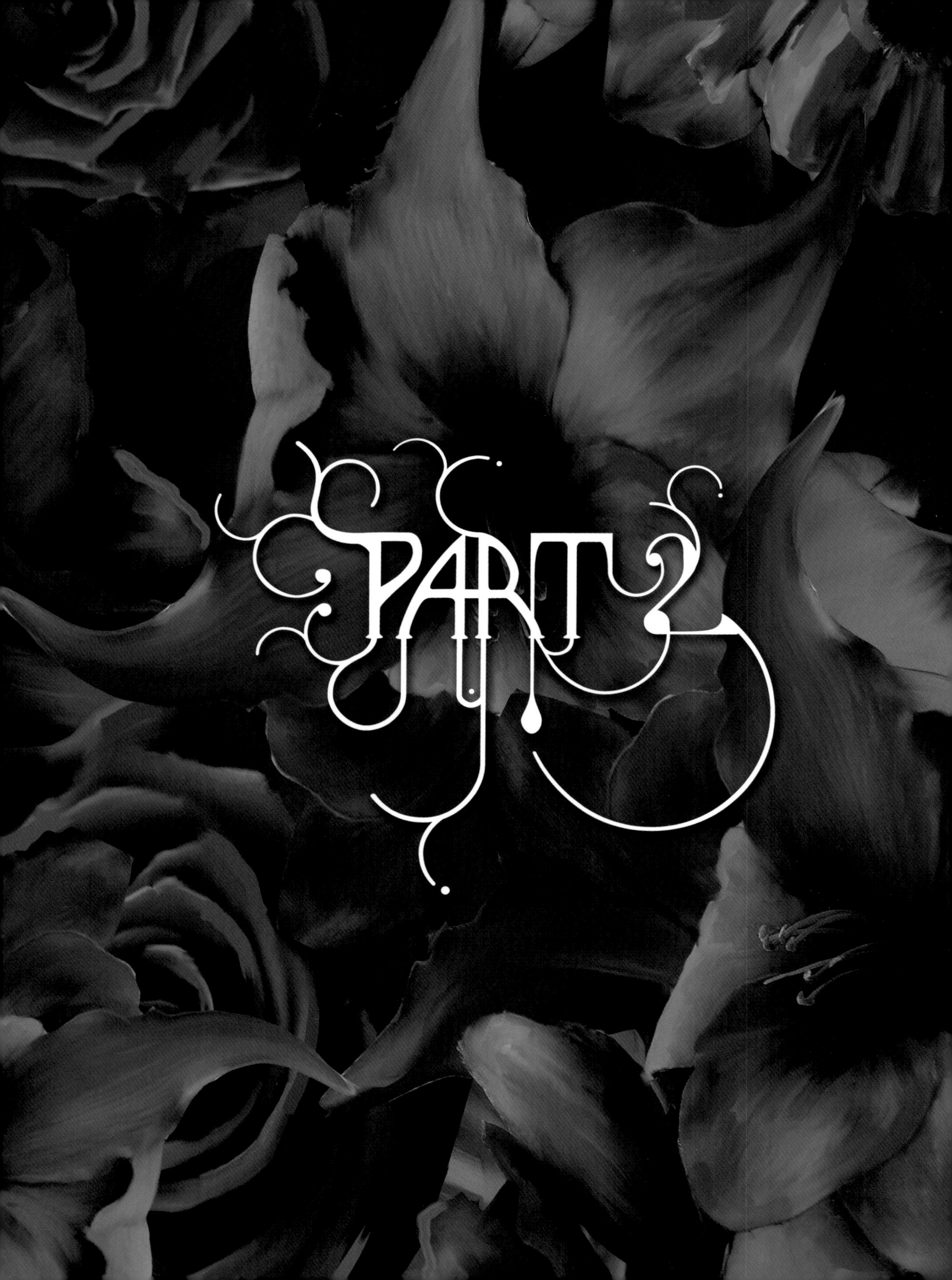

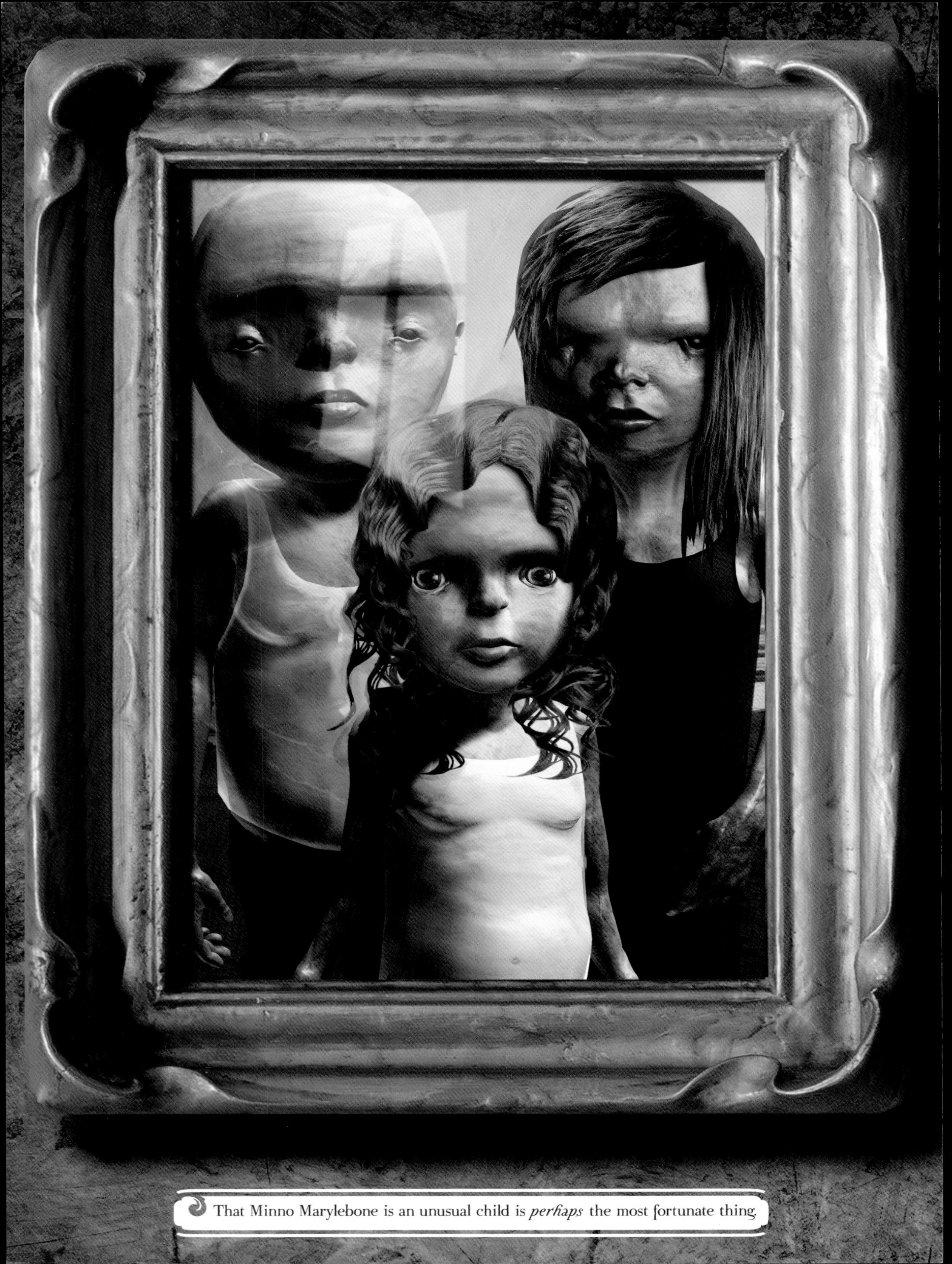

That Minno Marylebone is an unusual child is *perhaps* the most fortunate thing.

Minno Marylebone comes to the grounds every night.

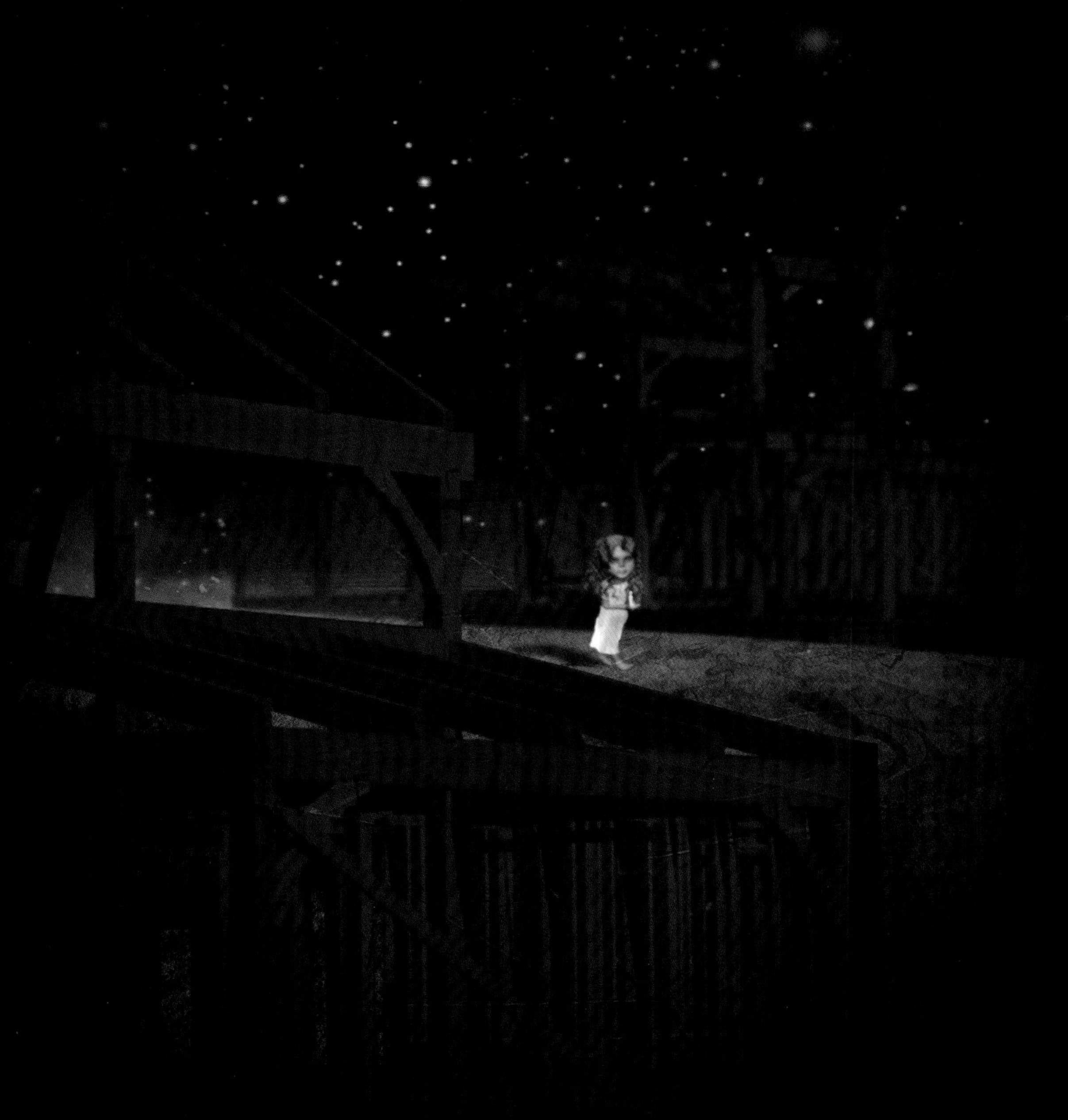

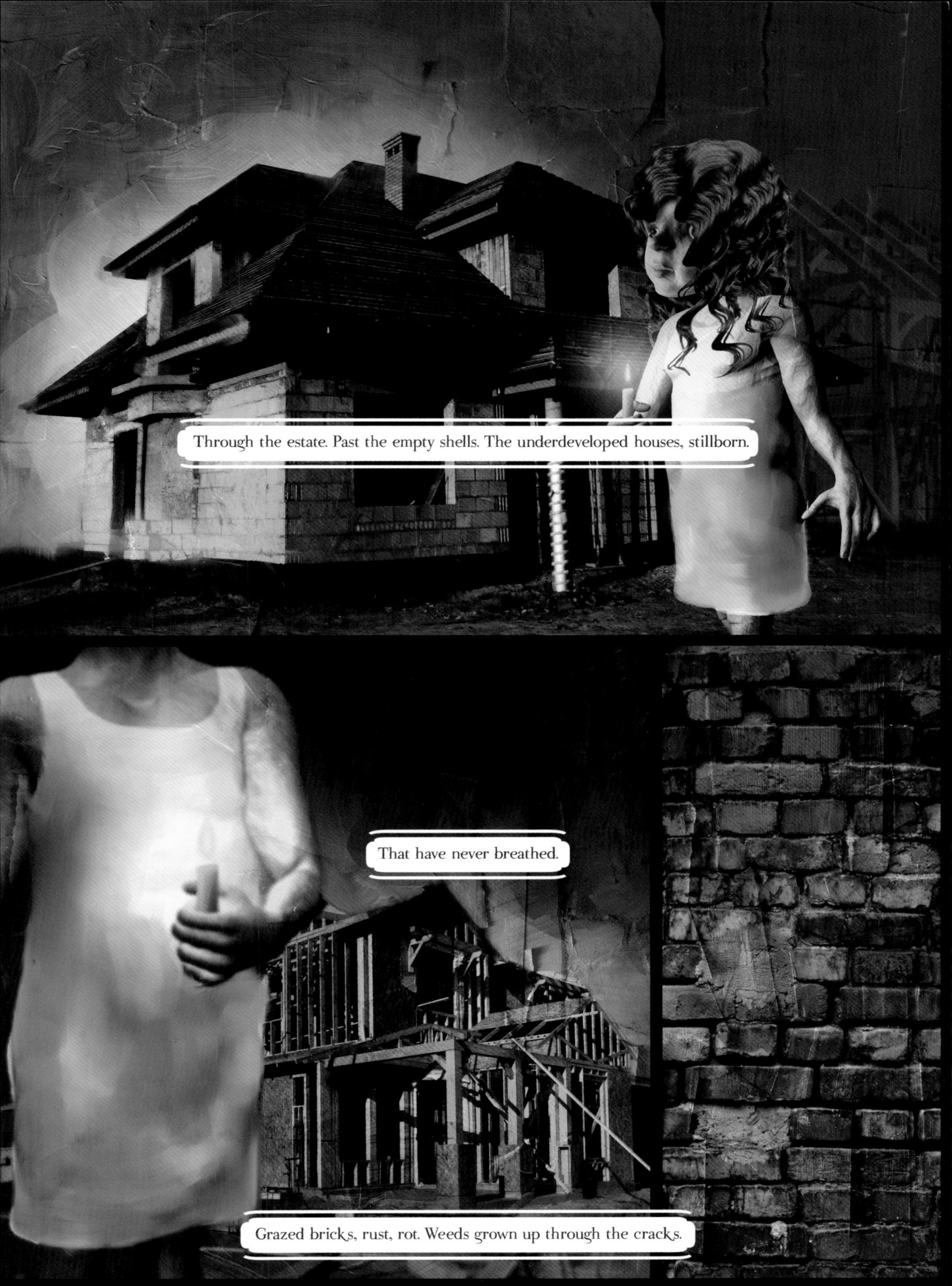
Through the estate. Past the empty shells. The underdeveloped houses, stillborn.
That have never breathed.
Grazed bricks, rust, rot. Weeds grown up through the cracks.

The child does not loiter. Does not play. Is unconcerned with the languid trappings of this ghost town.

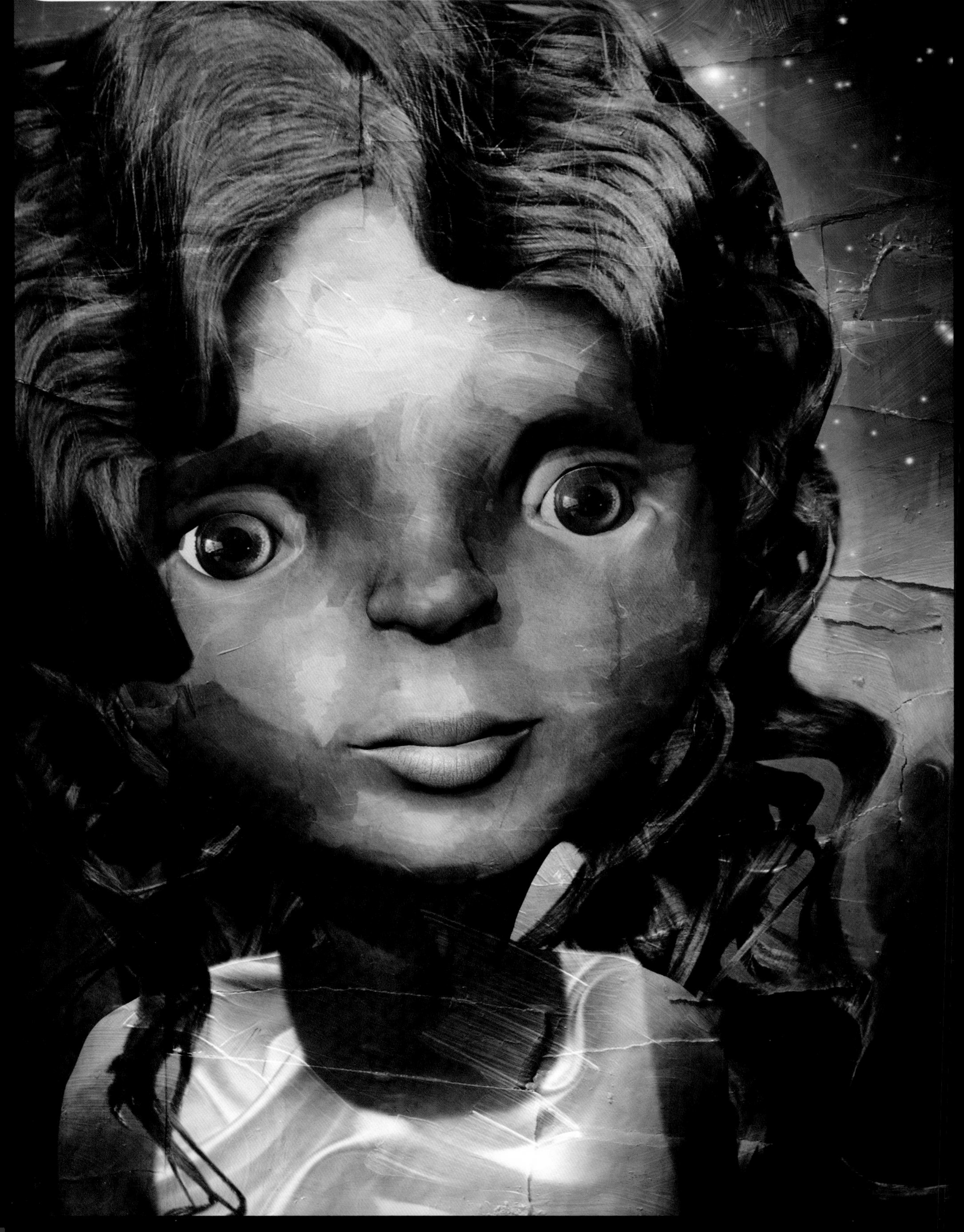

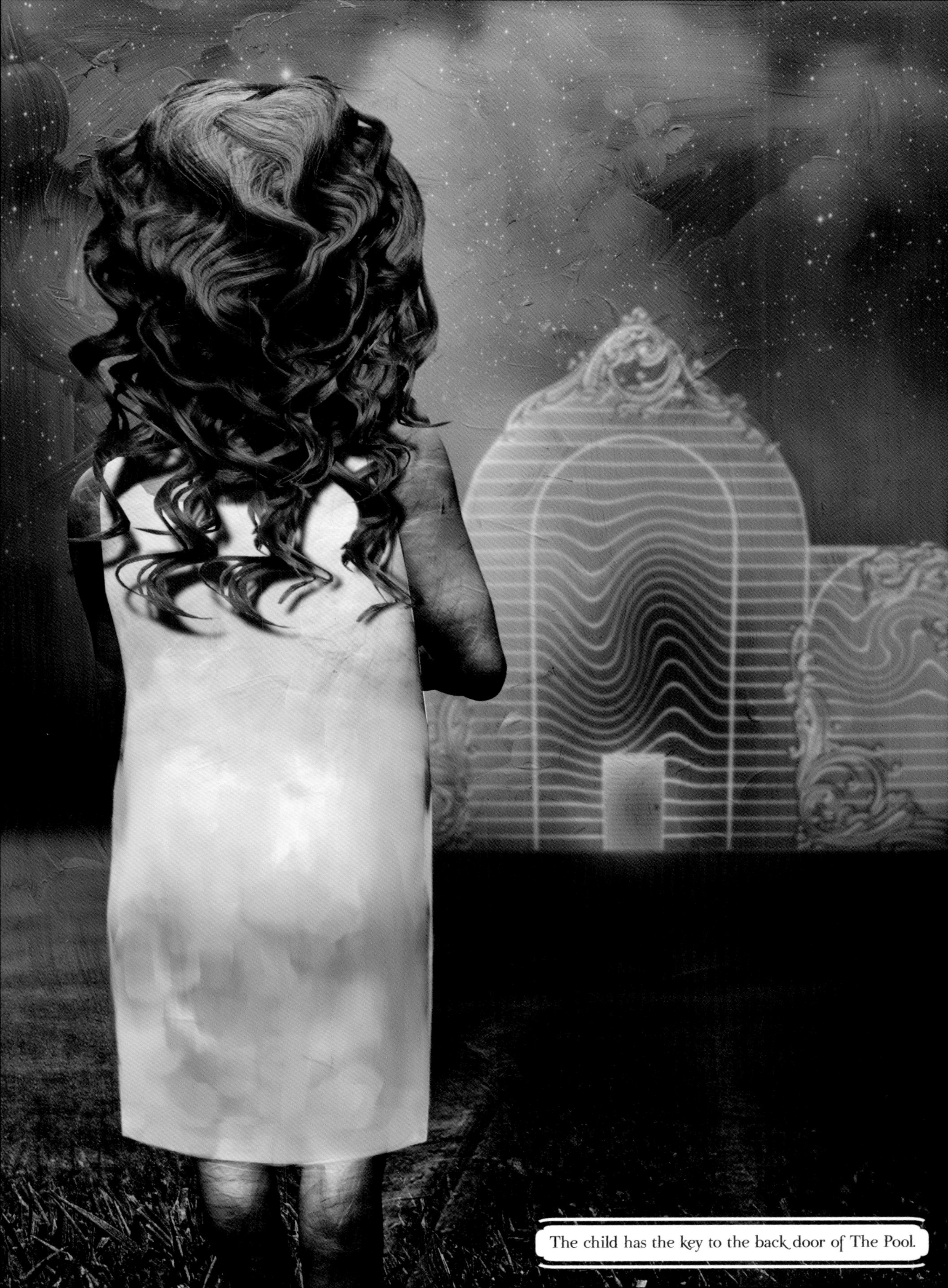

The child has the key to the back door of The Pool.

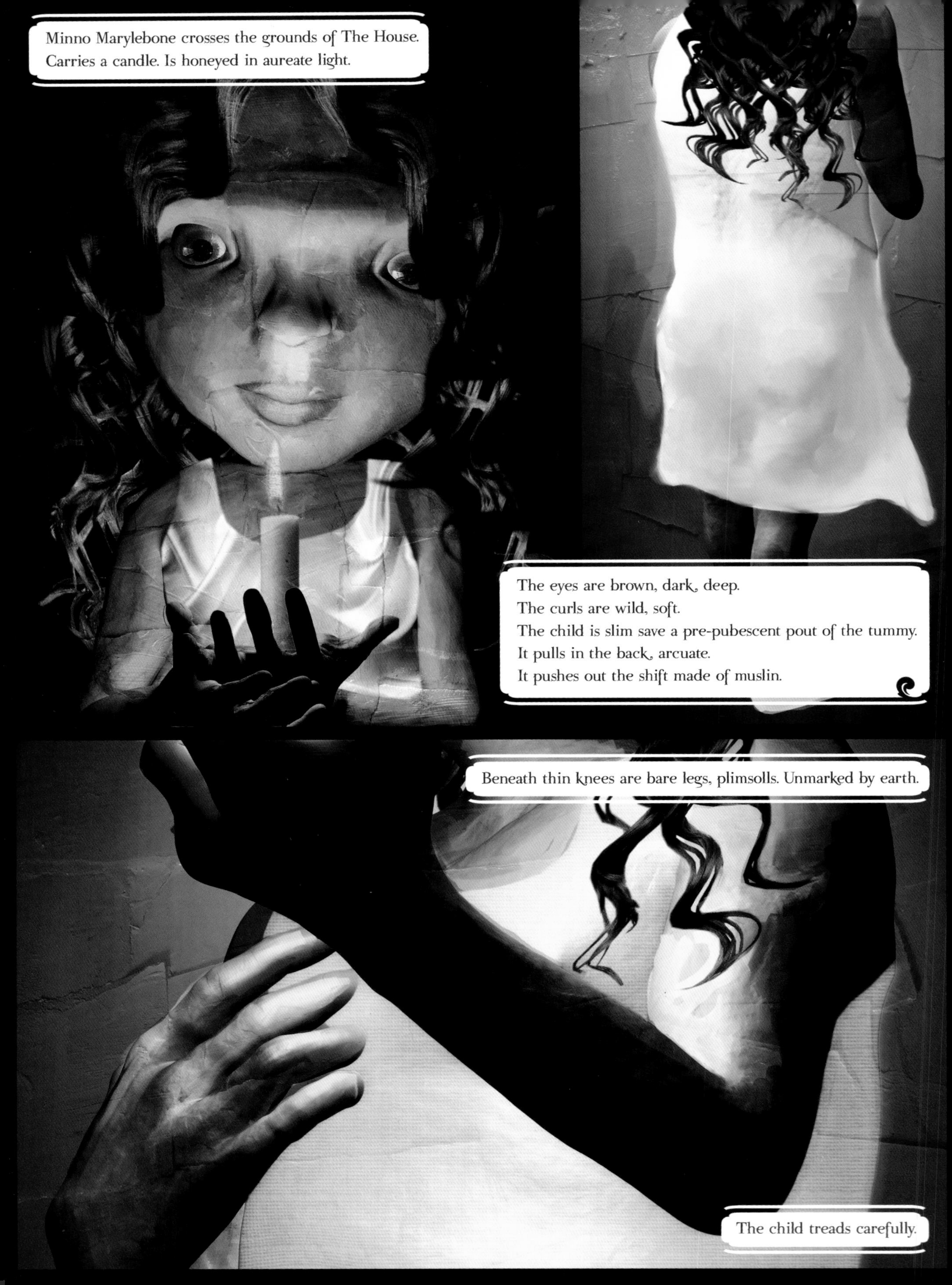
Minno Marylebone crosses the grounds of The House. Carries a candle. Is honeyed in aureate light.
The eyes are brown, dark, deep.
The curls are wild, soft.
The child is slim save a pre-pubescent pout of the tummy.
It pulls in the back, arcuate.
It pushes out the shift made of muslin.
Beneath thin knees are bare legs, plimsolls. Unmarked by earth.
The child treads carefully.

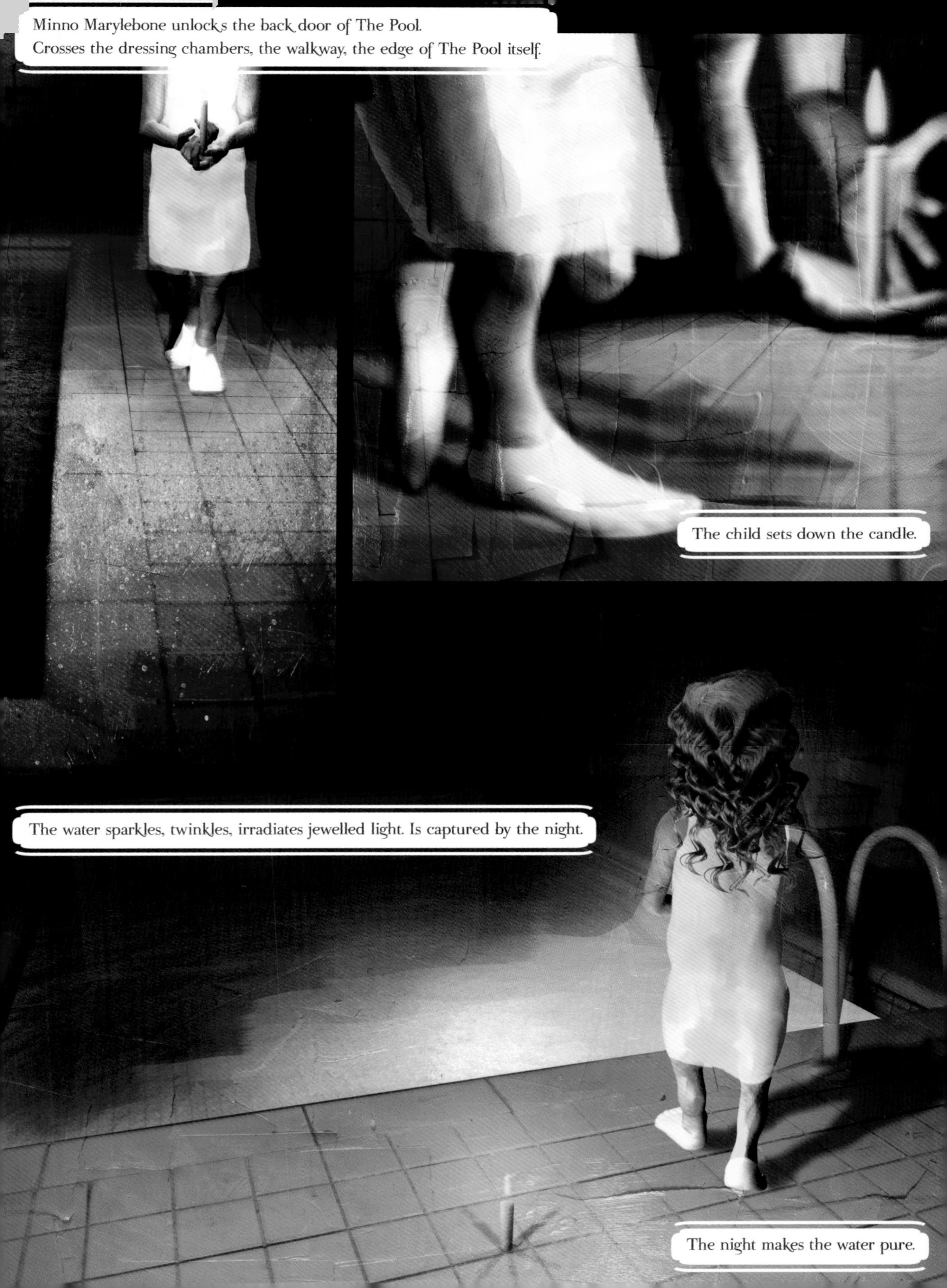
Minno Marylebone unlocks the back door of The Pool.
Crosses the dressing chambers, the walkway, the edge of The Pool itself.
The child sets down the candle.
The water sparkles, twinkles, irradiates jewelled light. Is captured by the night.
The night makes the water pure.

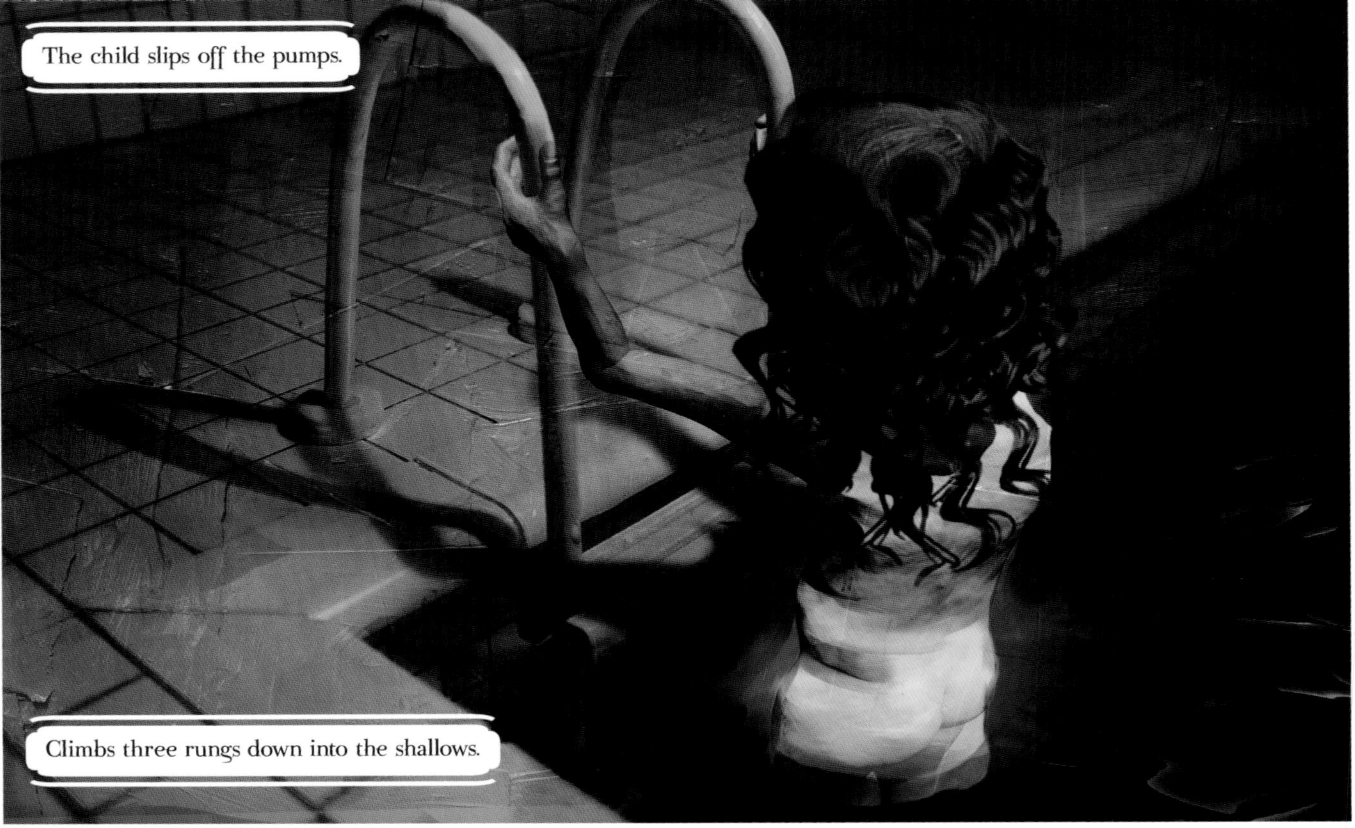
The child slips off the pumps.
Climbs three rungs down into the shallows.
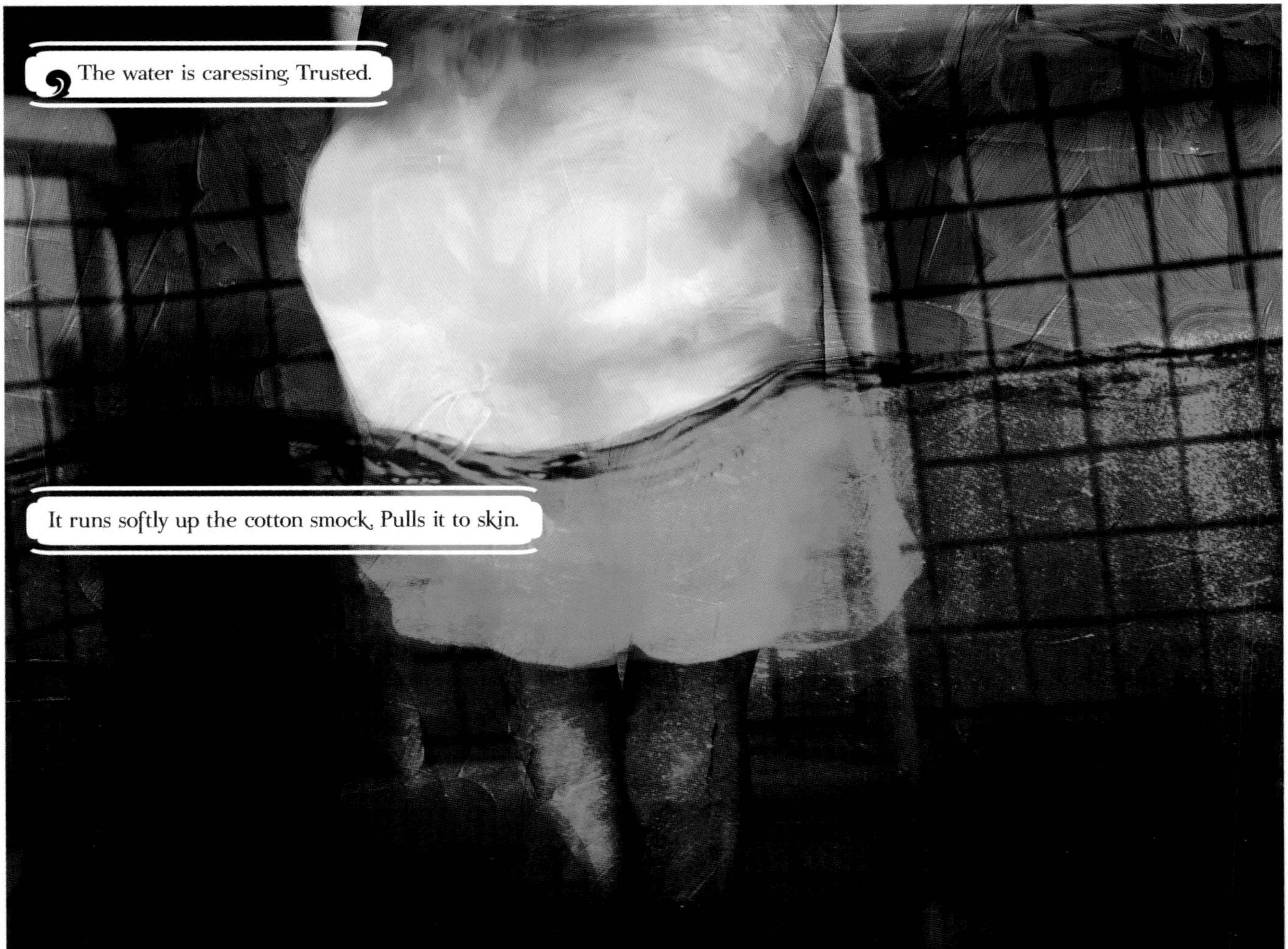
The water is caressing. Trusted.
It runs softly up the cotton smock. Pulls it to skin.

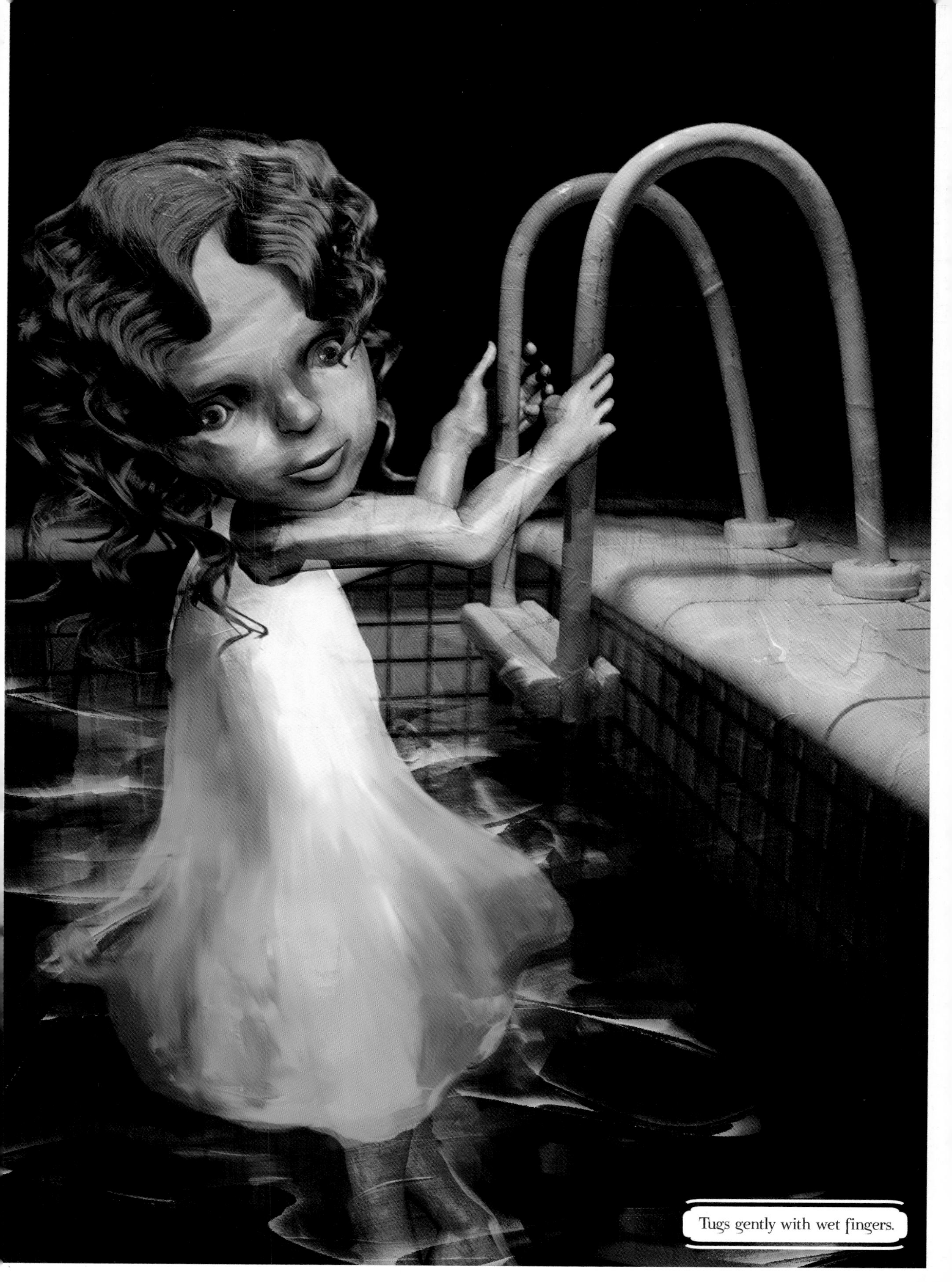

Tugs gently with wet fingers.

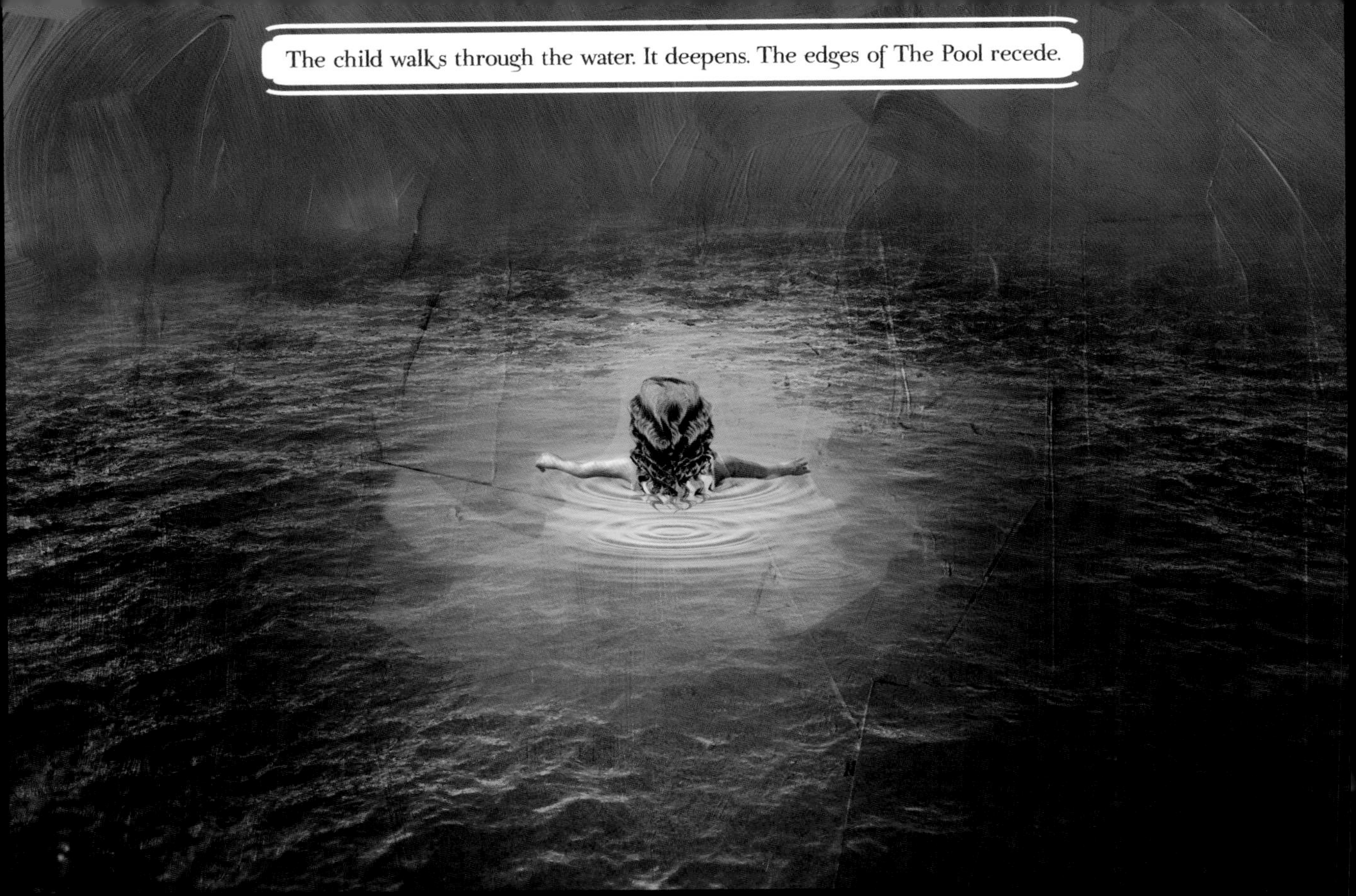
The child walks through the water. It deepens. The edges of The Pool recede.

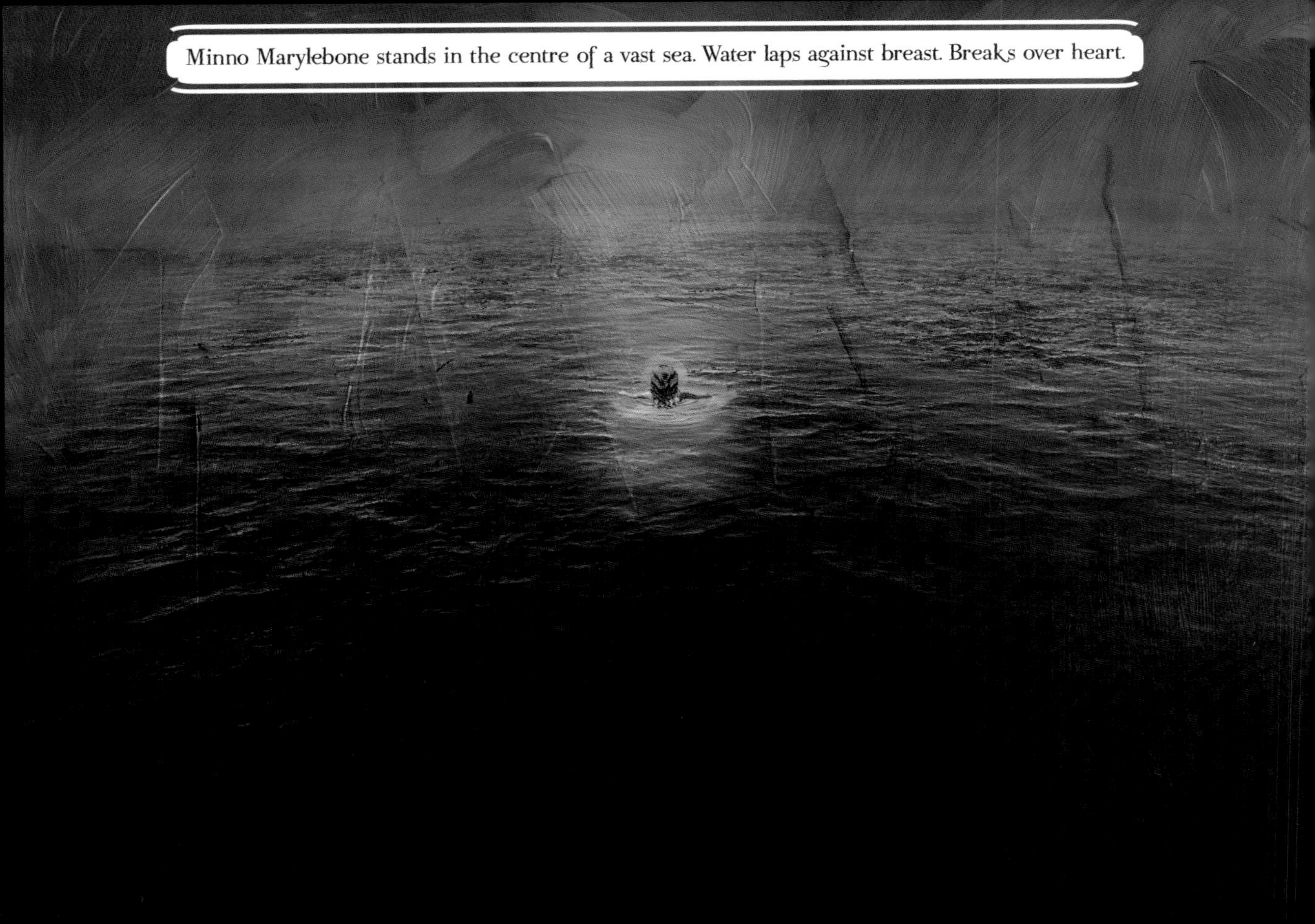
Minno Marylebone stands in the centre of a vast sea. Water laps against breast. Breaks over heart.

The child lifts wet hands, crosses arms, slender. Closes eyes and bows head. Statuesque.

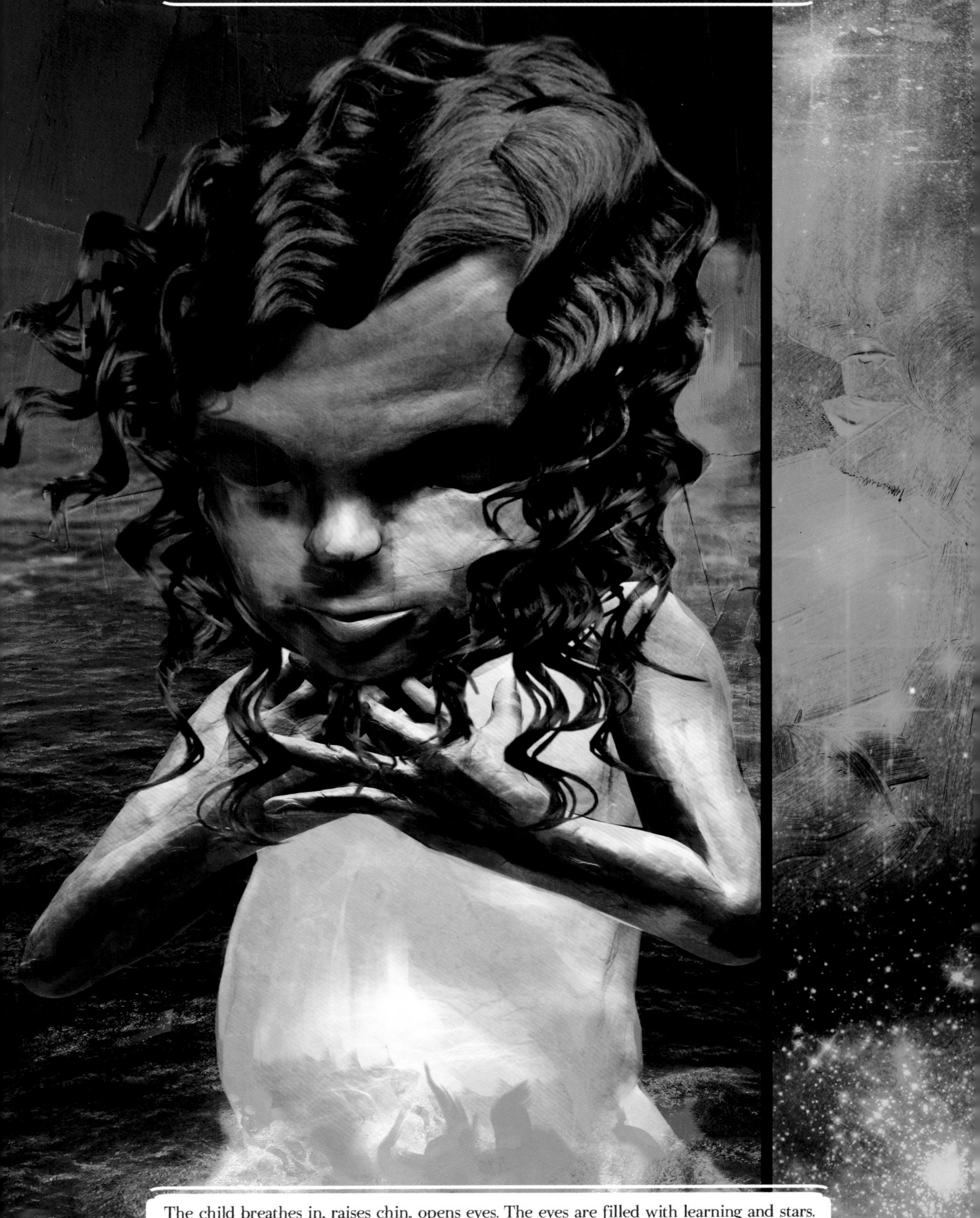

The child breathes in, raises chin, opens eyes. The eyes are filled with learning and stars. Eleven shades of gold.

Minno Marylebone falls backwards. The fall goes on forever. Water is coming and kissing the child. On cheeks, on lids, on lips. Pouring in the dark deep eyes. Flowing through. Filling everything. Cleansing, completing.

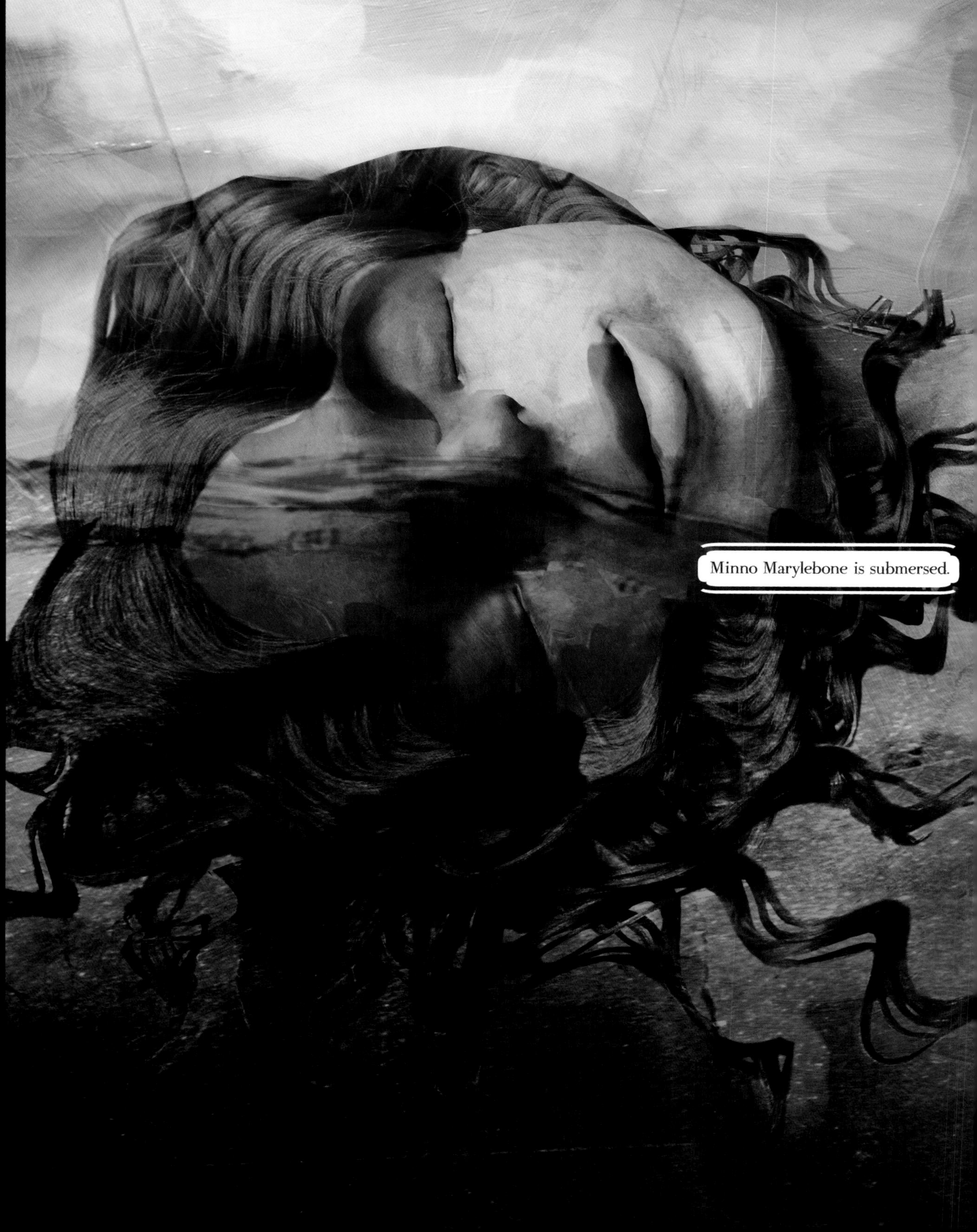

Minno Marylebone is submersed.

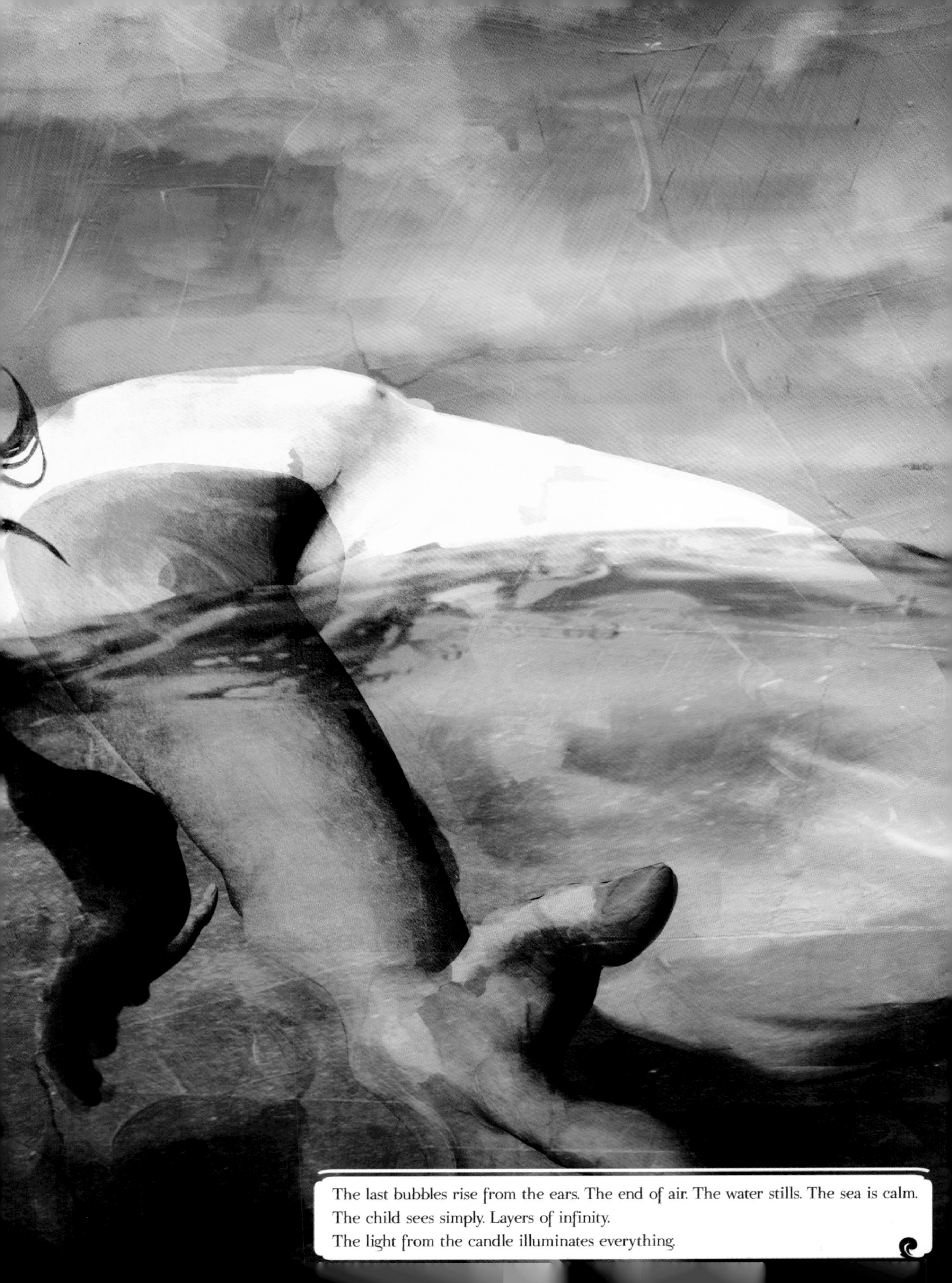

The last bubbles rise from the ears. The end of air. The water stills. The sea is calm.
The child sees simply. Layers of infinity.
The light from the candle illuminates everything.

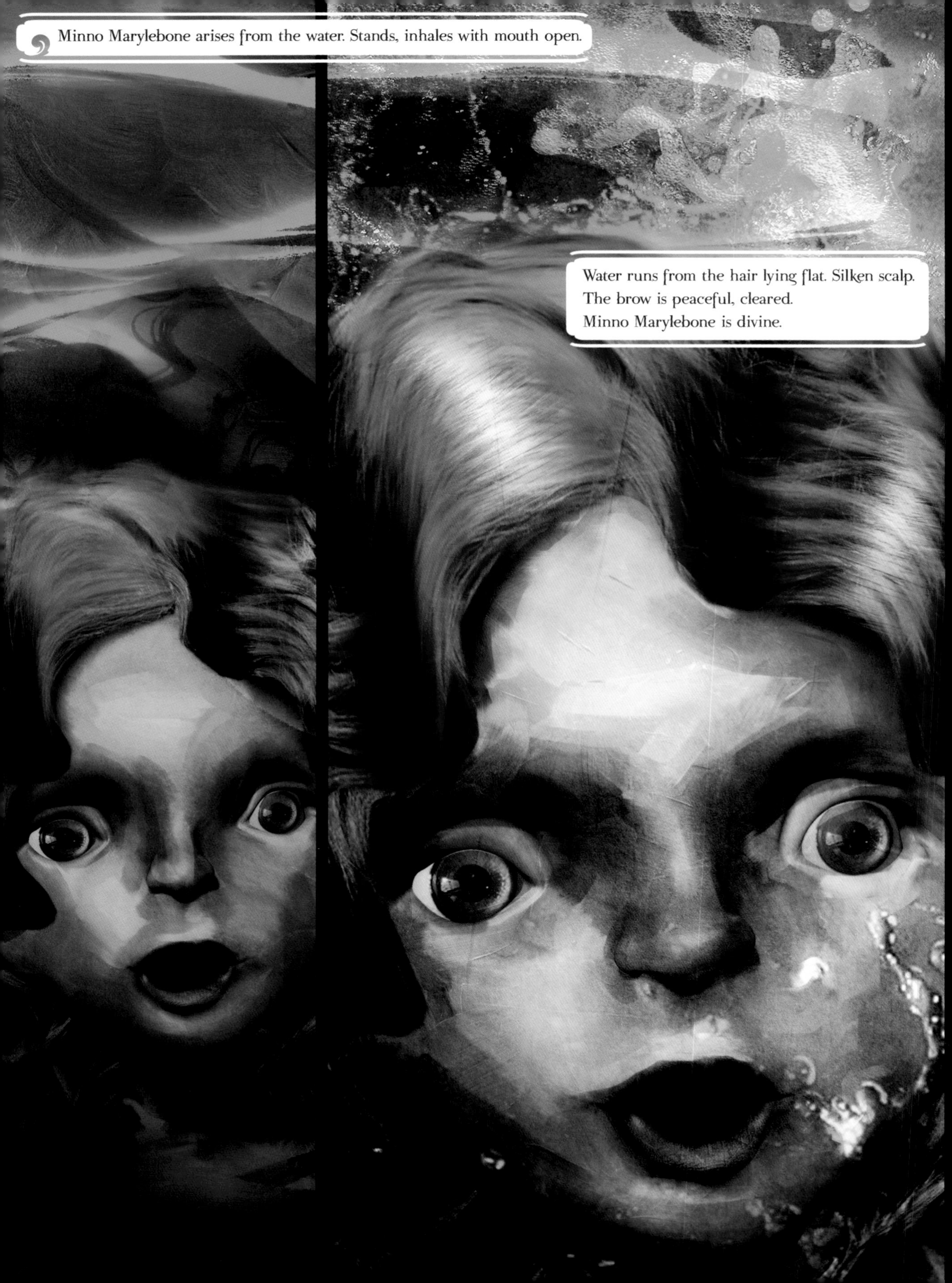
Minno Marylebone arises from the water. Stands, inhales with mouth open.
Water runs from the hair lying flat. Silken scalp. The brow is peaceful, cleared. Minno Marylebone is divine.

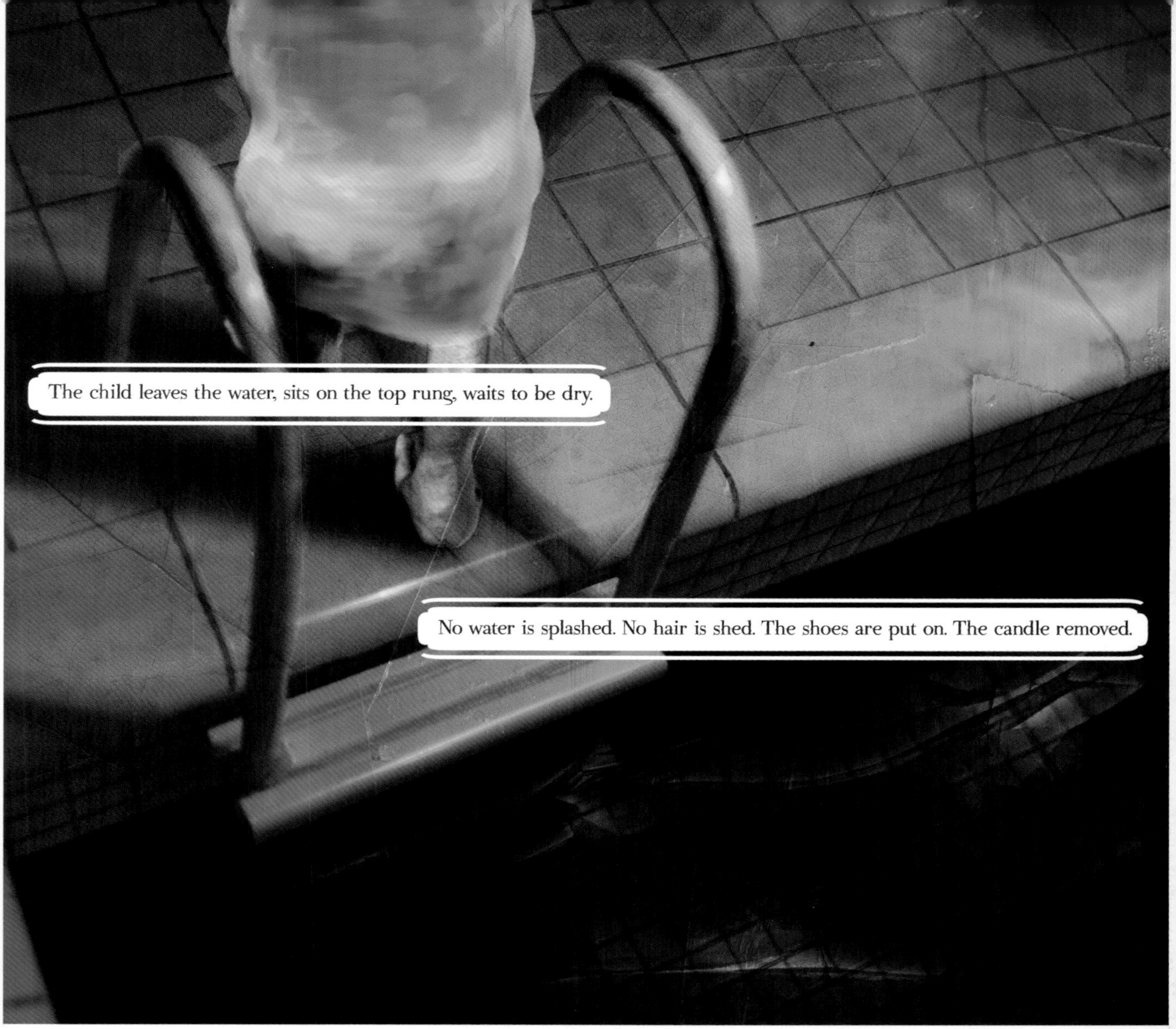
The child leaves the water, sits on the top rung, waits to be dry.
No water is splashed. No hair is shed. The shoes are put on. The candle removed.

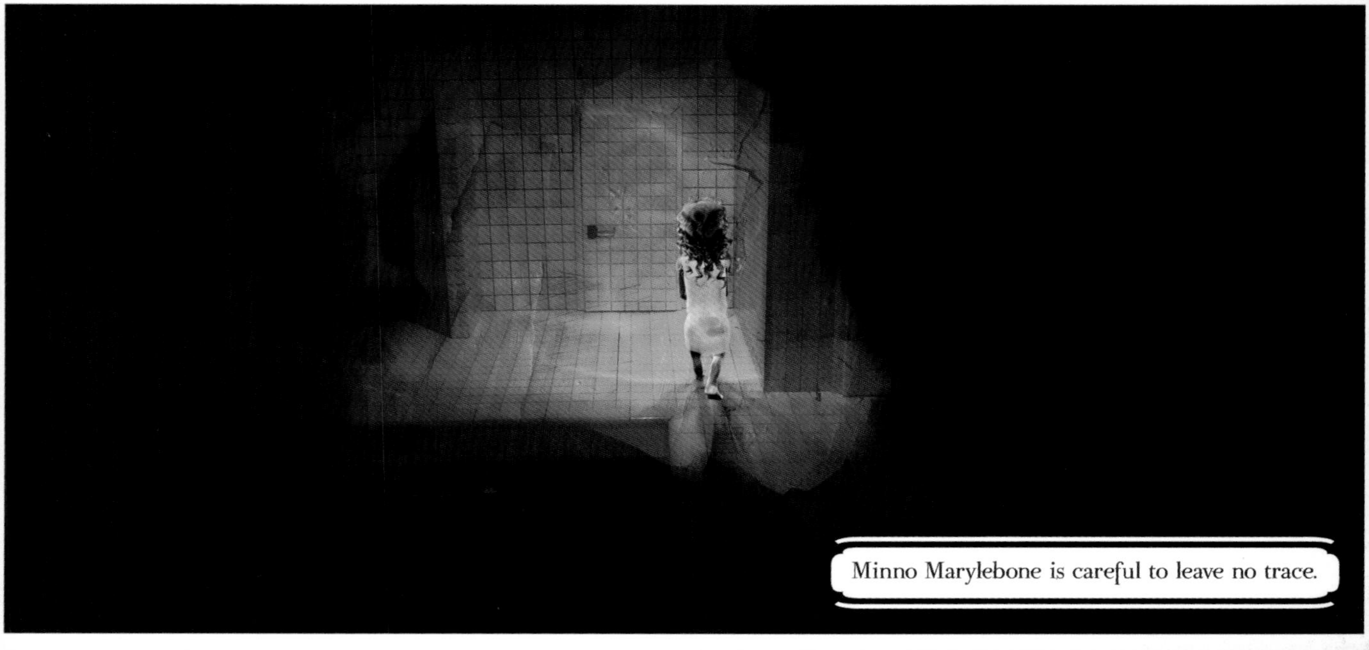
Minno Marylebone is careful to leave no trace.

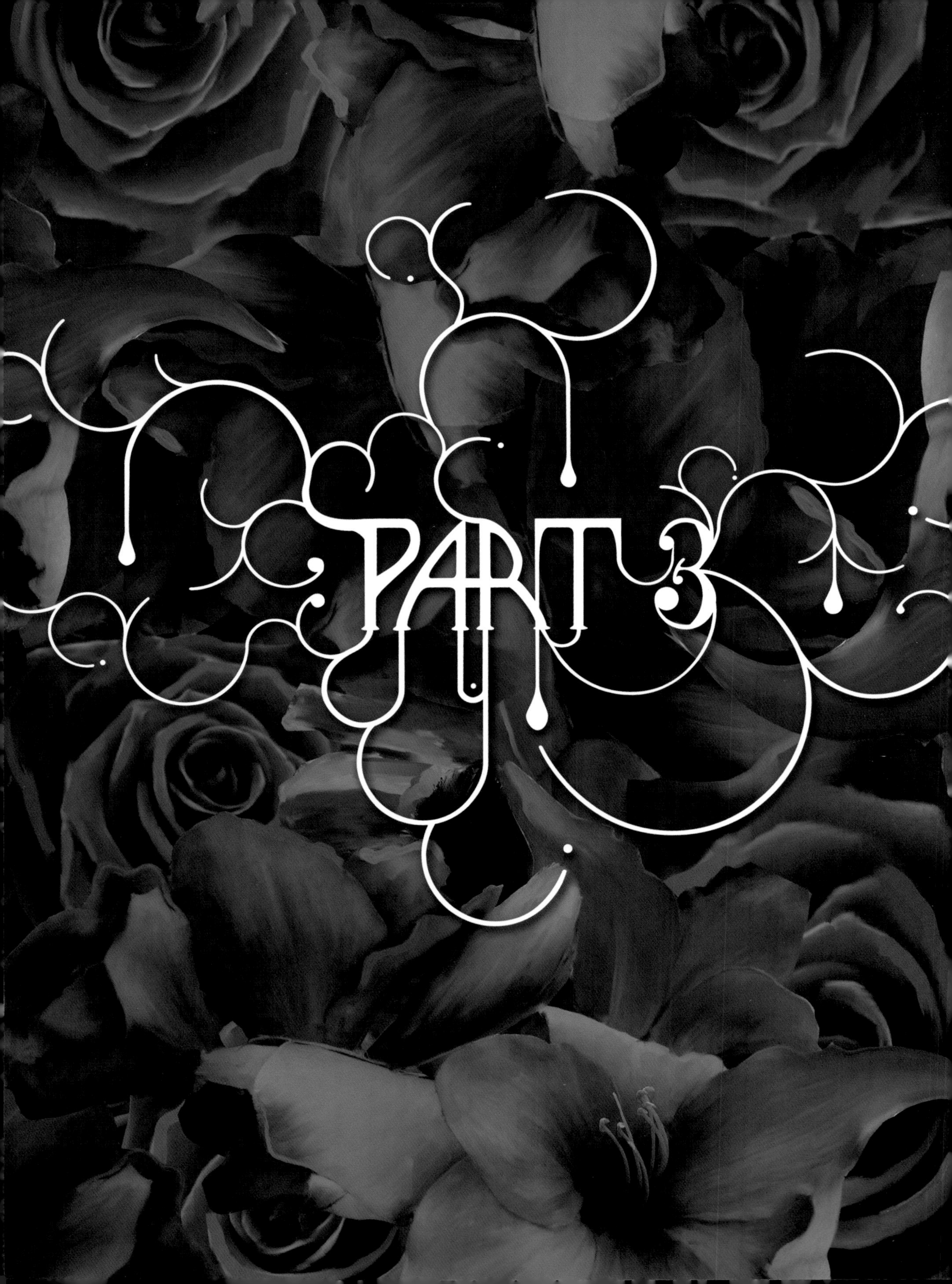
PART 3

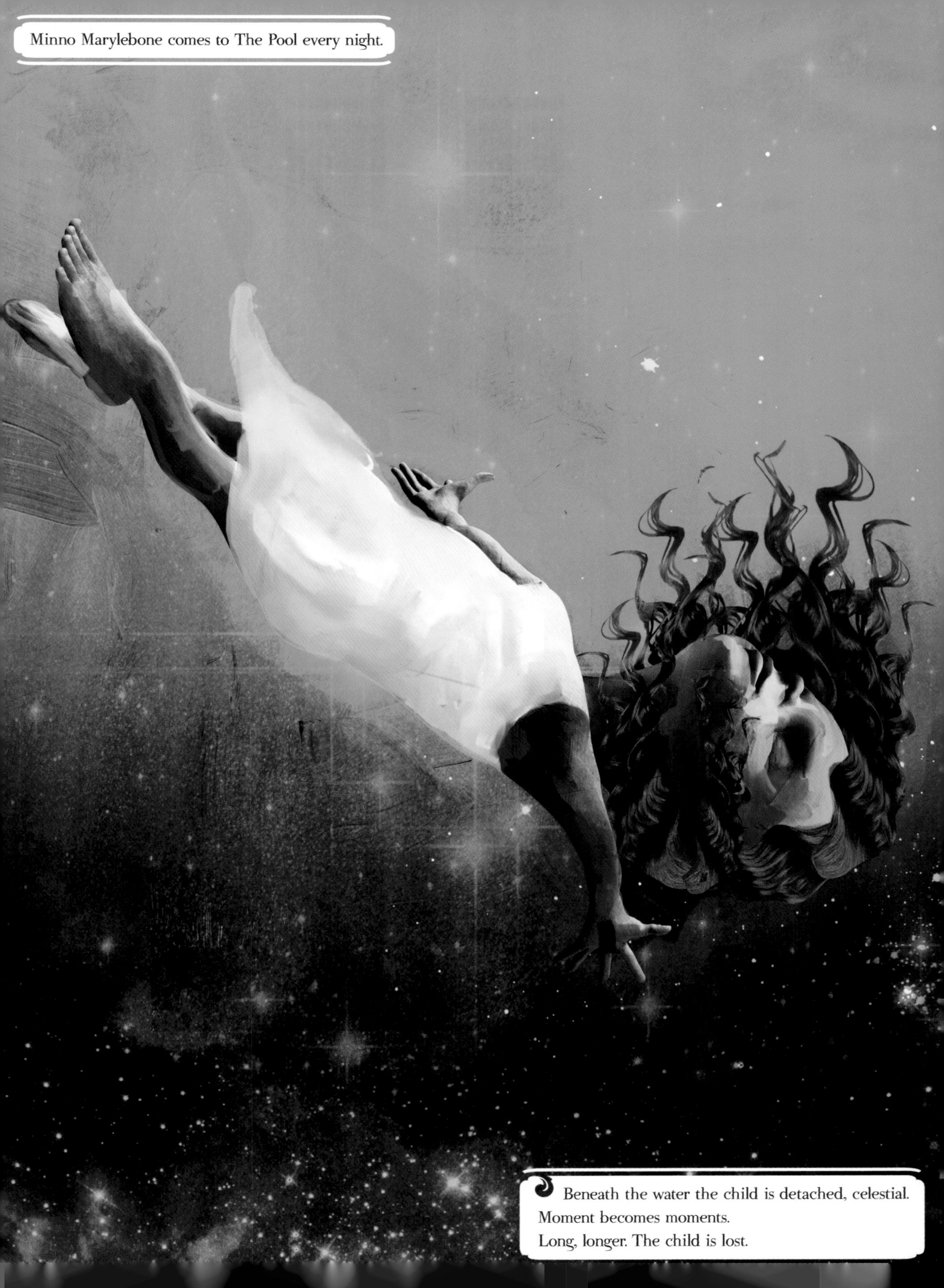
Minno Marylebone comes to The Pool every night.
Beneath the water the child is detached, celestial.
Moment becomes moments.
Long, longer. The child is lost.

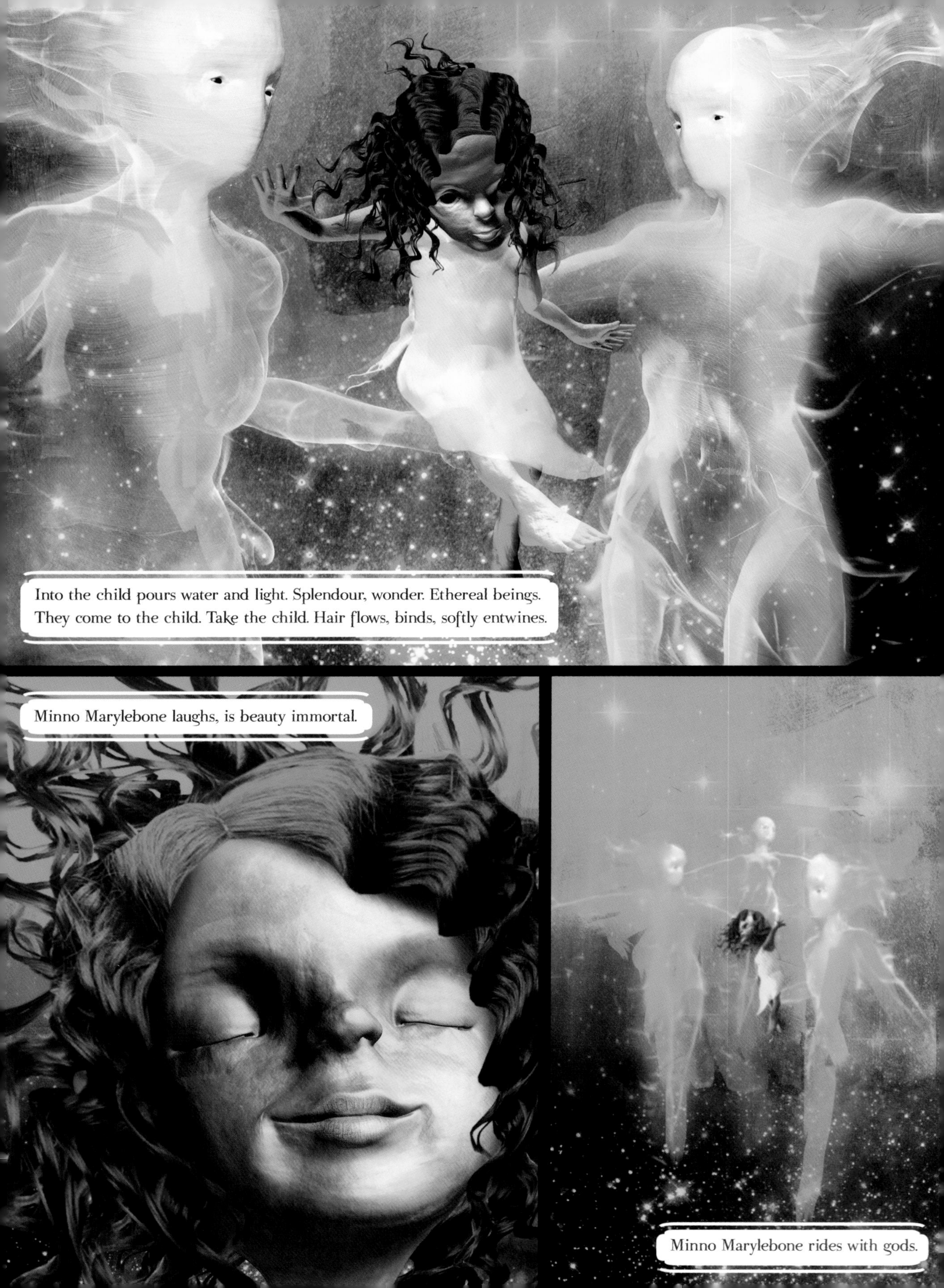
Into the child pours water and light. Splendour, wonder. Ethereal beings. They come to the child. Take the child. Hair flows, binds, softly entwines.
Minno Marylebone laughs, is beauty immortal.
Minno Marylebone rides with gods.

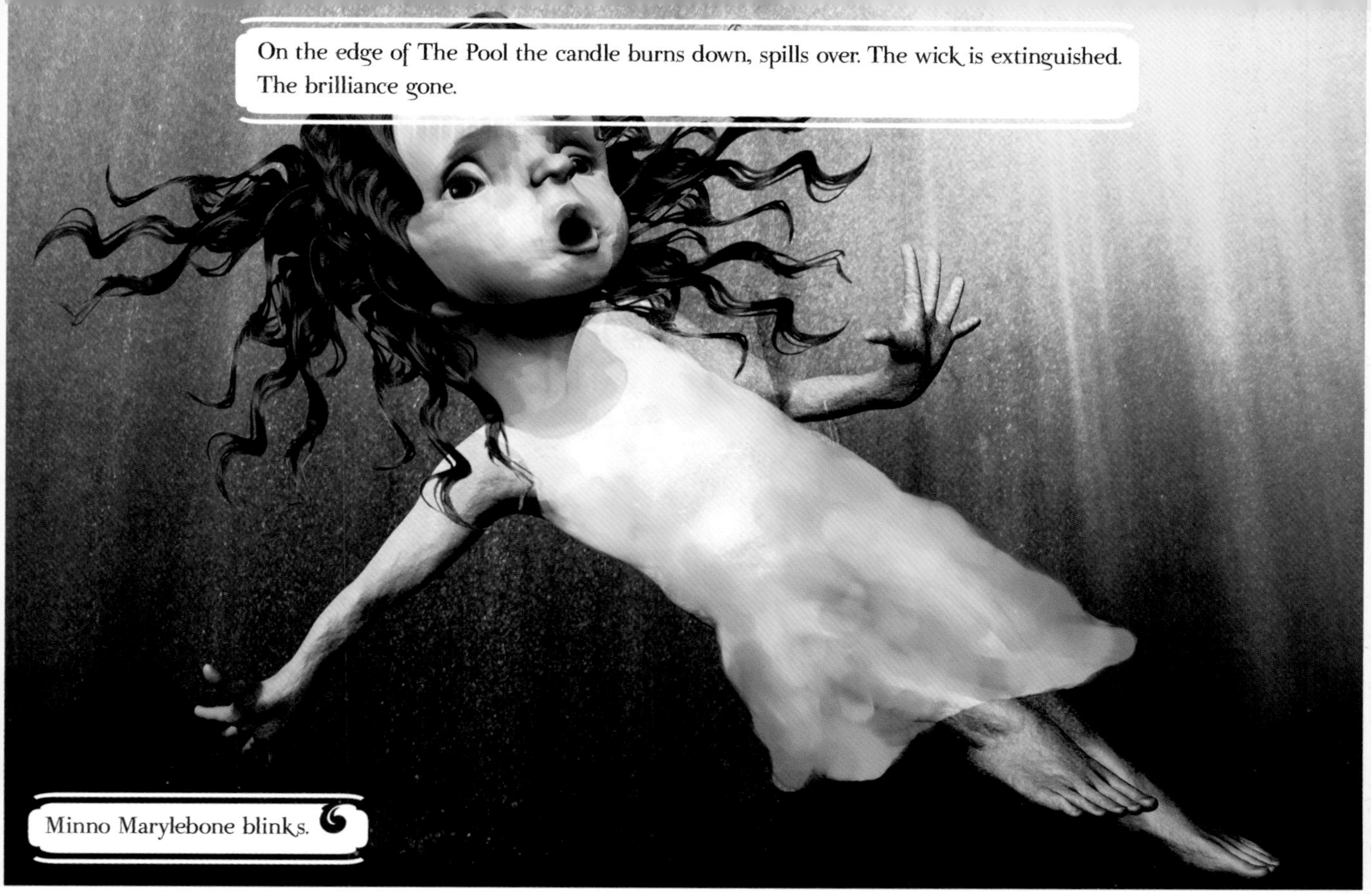
On the edge of The Pool the candle burns down, spills over. The wick is extinguished. The brilliance gone.
Minno Marylebone blinks.

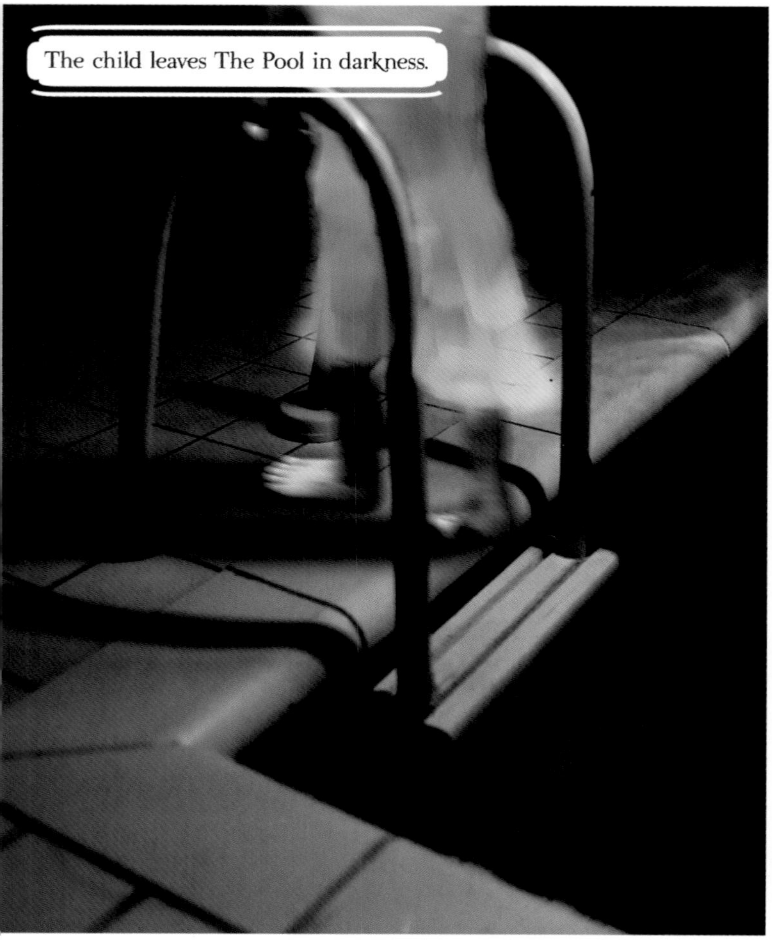
The child leaves The Pool in darkness.

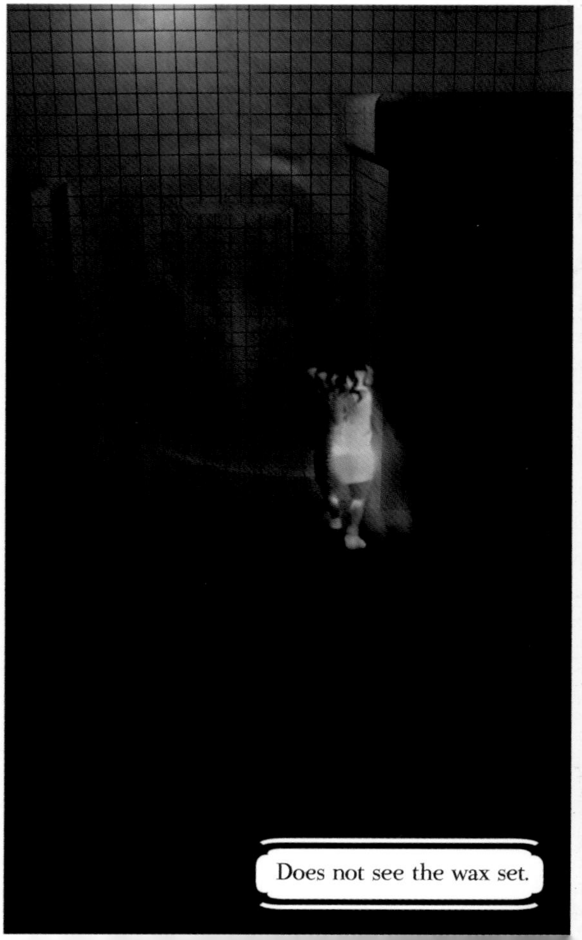
Does not see the wax set.

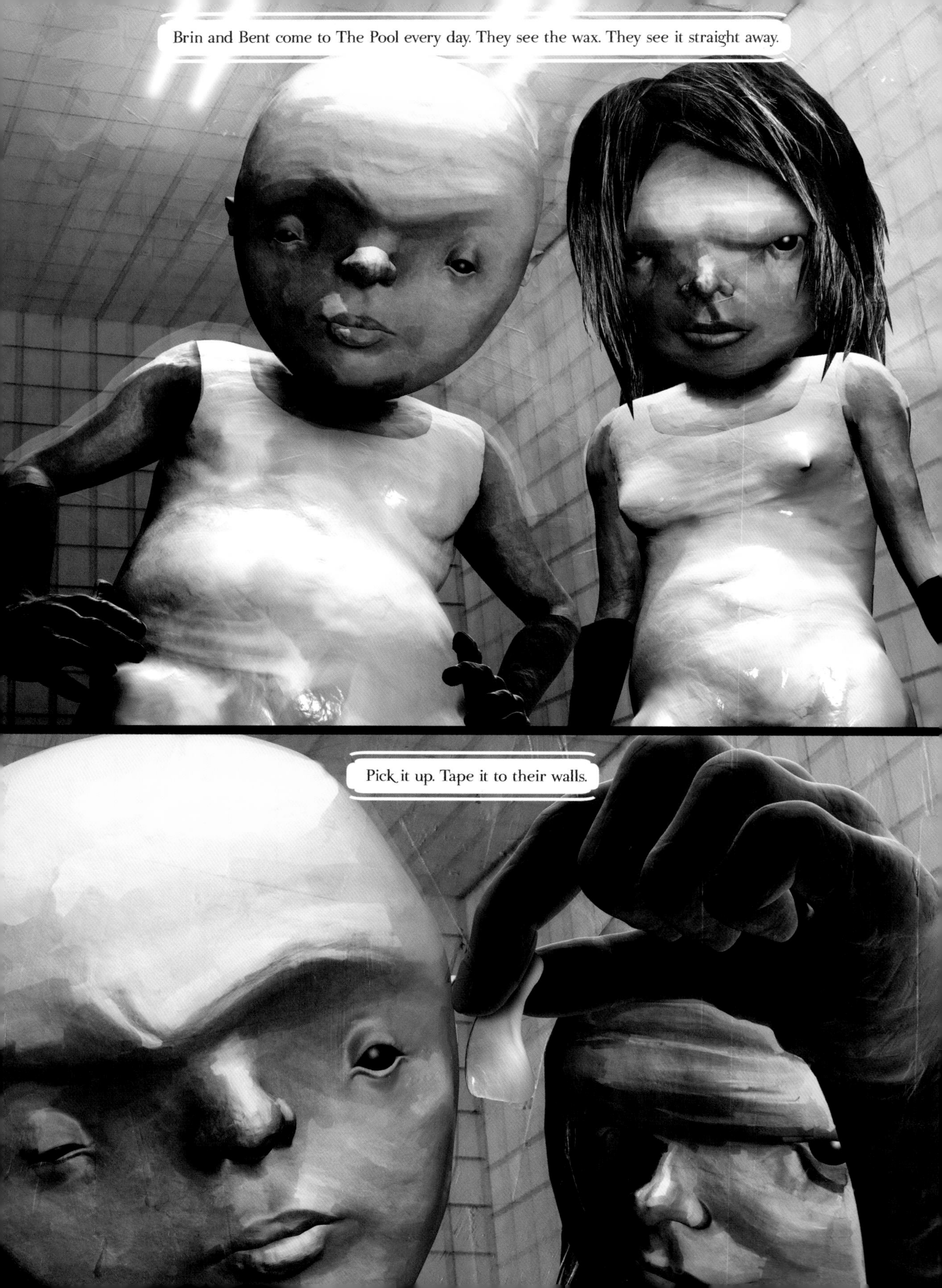
Brin and Bent come to The Pool every day. They see the wax. They see it straight away.
Pick it up. Tape it to their walls.

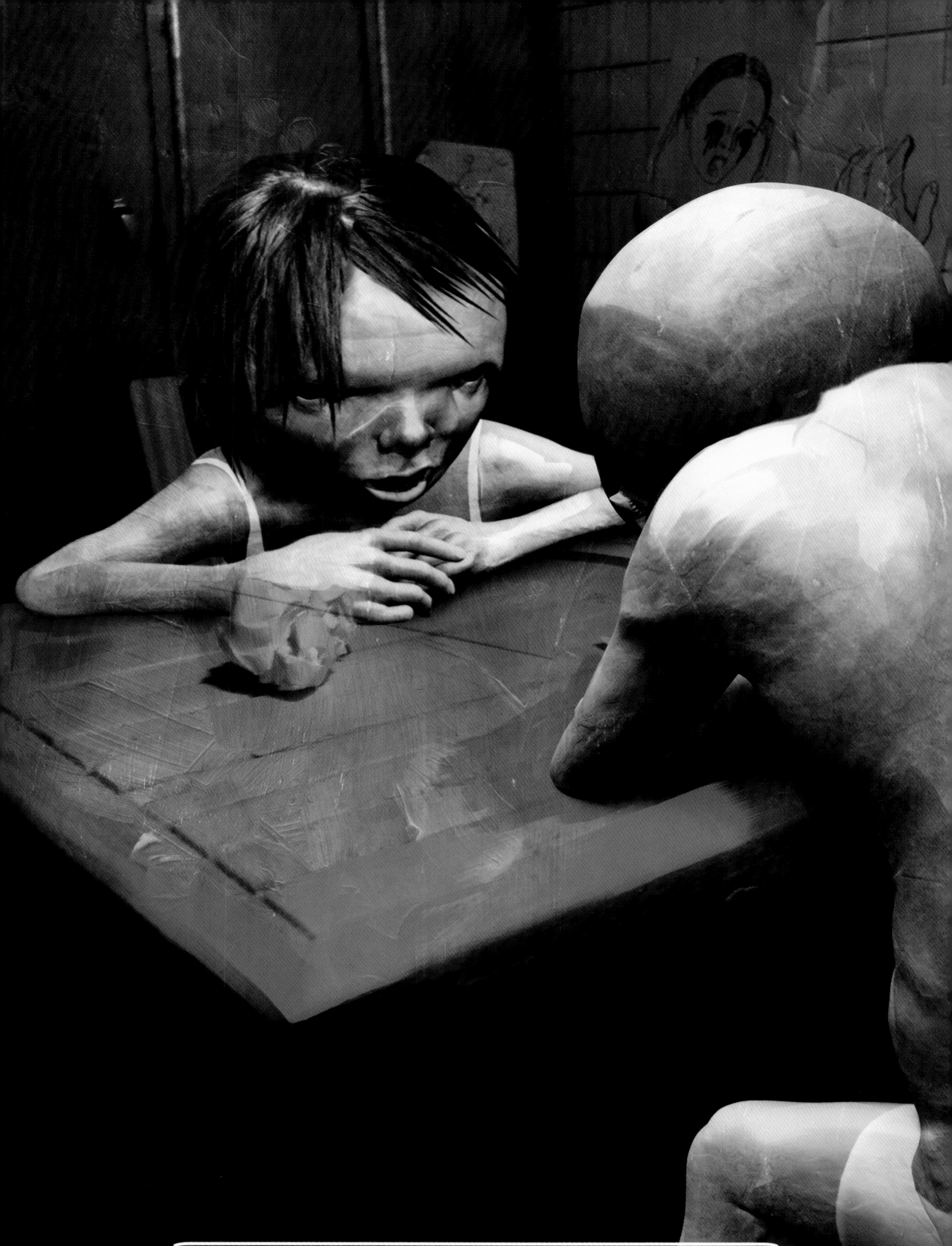

Thoughts come fast and curious. They wonder. All day long they tick and plot.

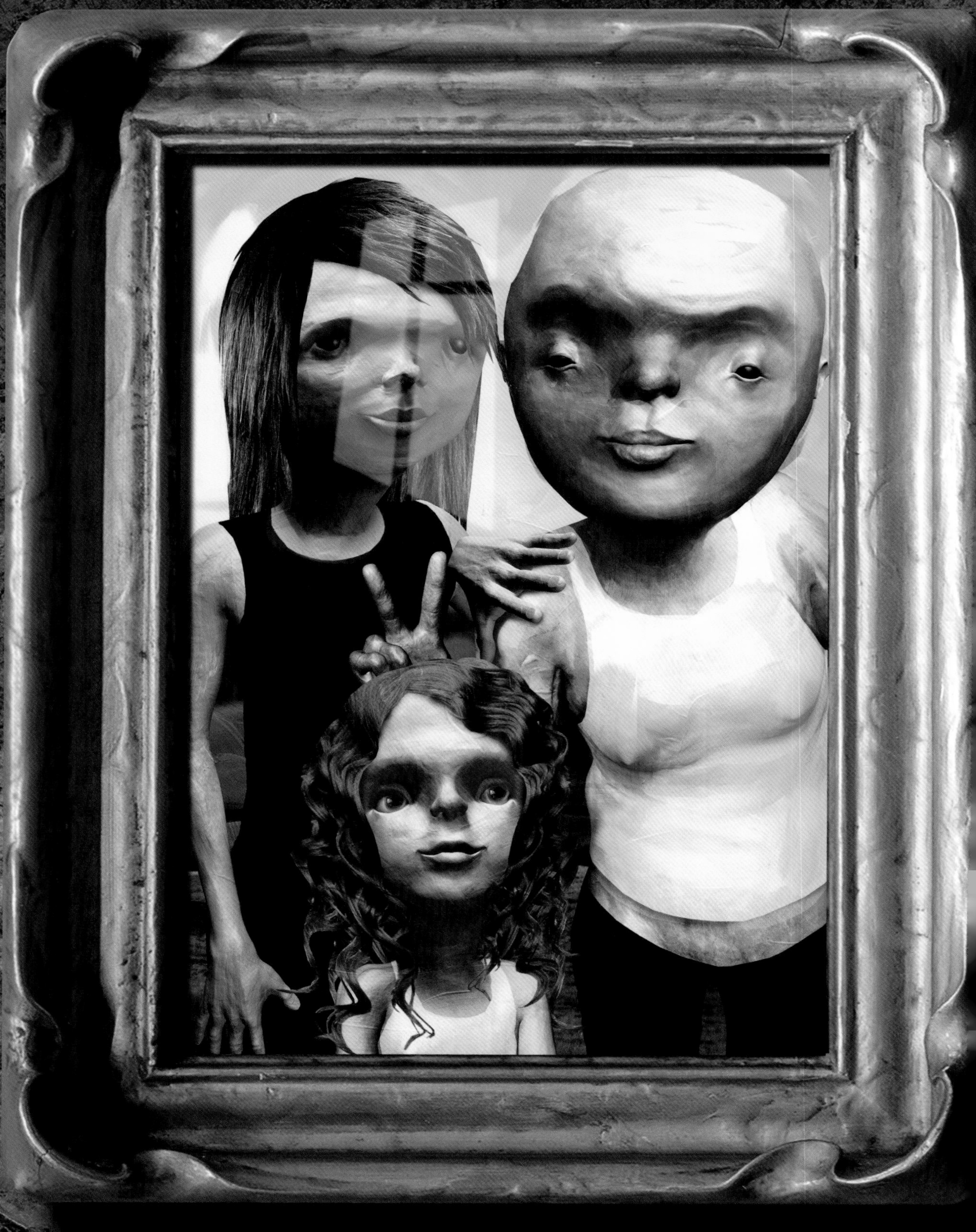

That Brin and Bent catch Minno Marylebone is *perhaps* the most fortunate thing.

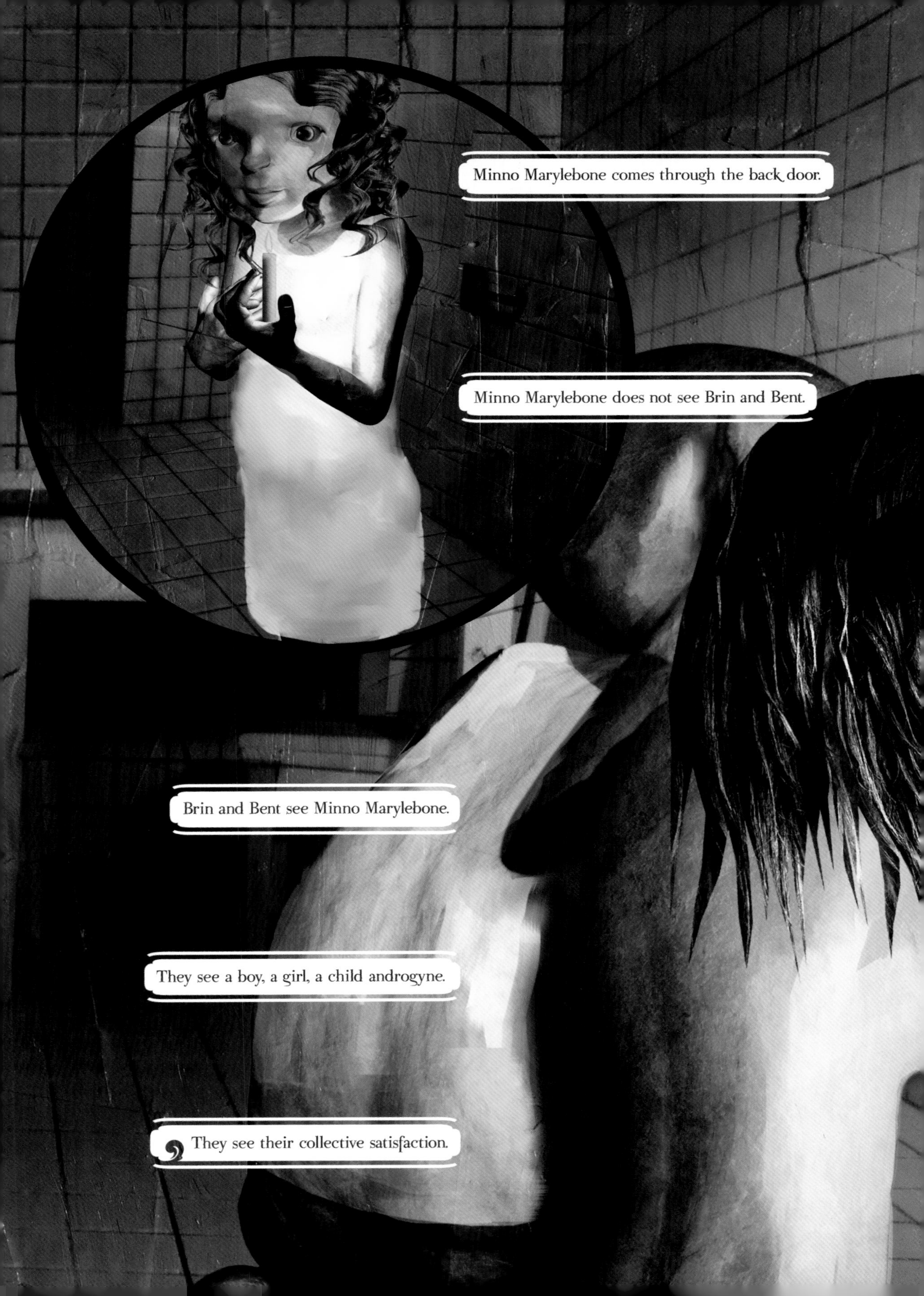
Minno Marylebone comes through the back door.
Minno Marylebone does not see Brin and Bent.
Brin and Bent see Minno Marylebone.
They see a boy, a girl, a child androgyne.
They see their collective satisfaction.

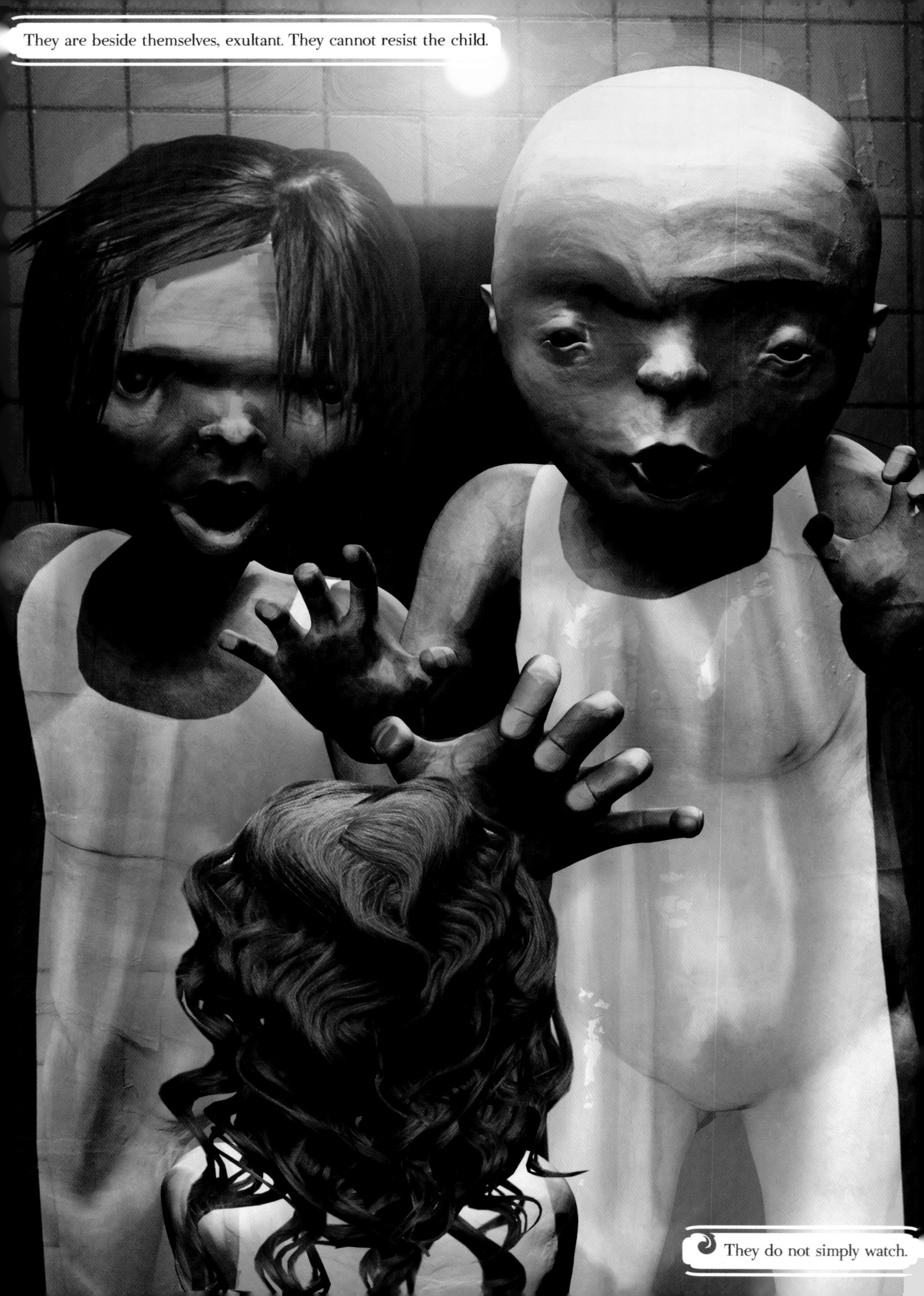
They are beside themselves, exultant. They cannot resist the child.
They do not simply watch.

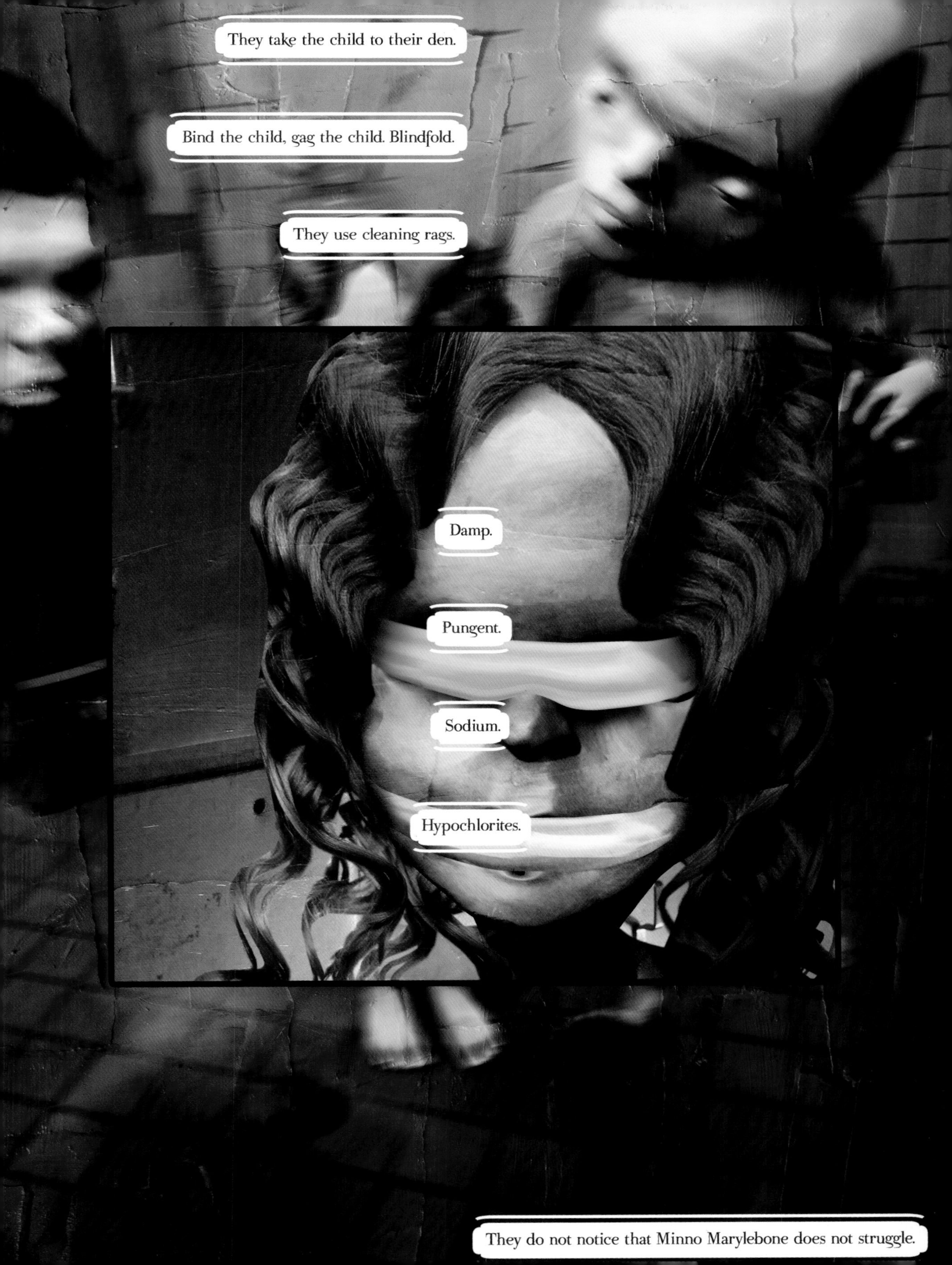
They take the child to their den.
Bind the child, gag the child. Blindfold.
They use cleaning rags.
Damp.
Pungent.
Sodium.
Hypochlorites.
They do not notice that Minno Marylebone does not struggle.

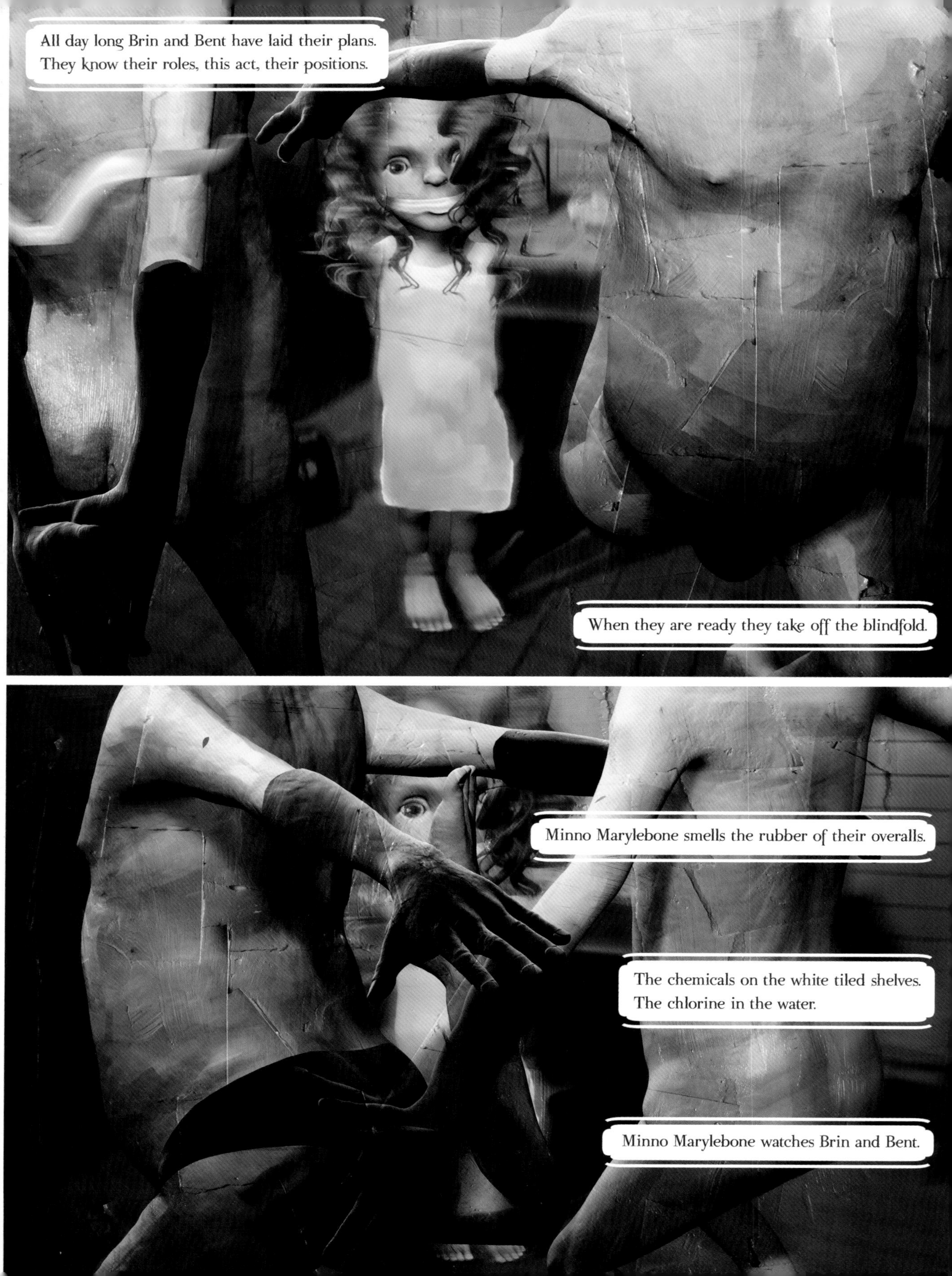
All day long Brin and Bent have laid their plans. They know their roles, this act, their positions.
When they are ready they take off the blindfold.
Minno Marylebone smells the rubber of their overalls.
The chemicals on the white tiled shelves. The chlorine in the water.
Minno Marylebone watches Brin and Bent.

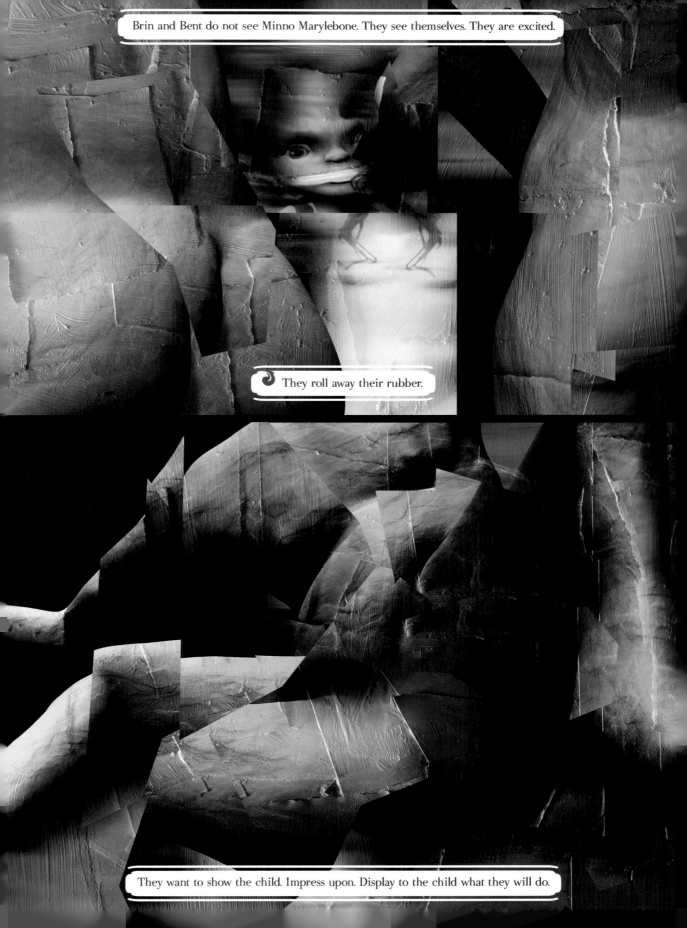

Brin and Bent do not see Minno Marylebone. They see themselves. They are excited.

They roll away their rubber.

They want to show the child. Impress upon. Display to the child what they will do.

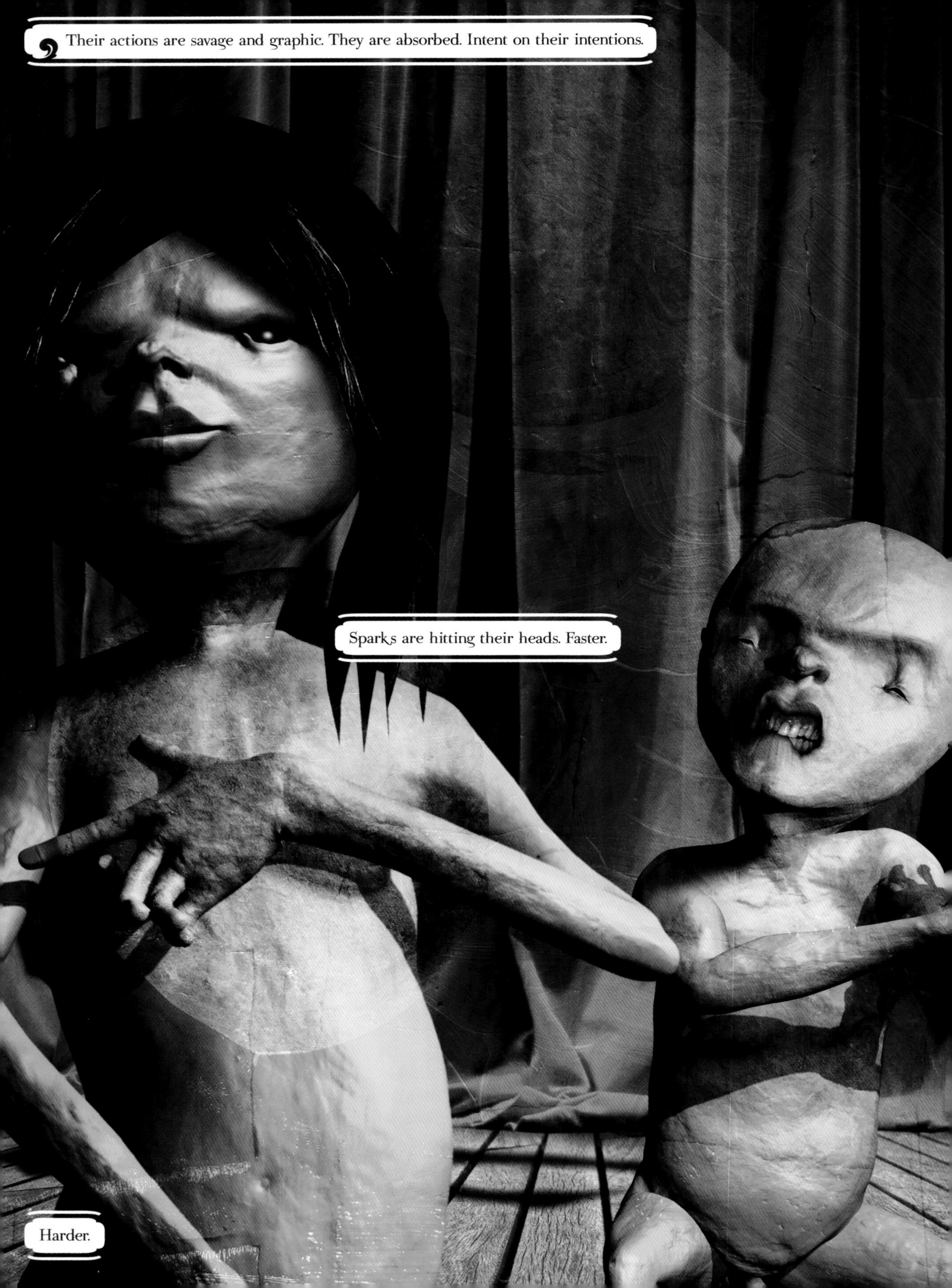
Their actions are savage and graphic. They are absorbed. Intent on their intentions.
Sparks are hitting their heads. Faster.
Harder.

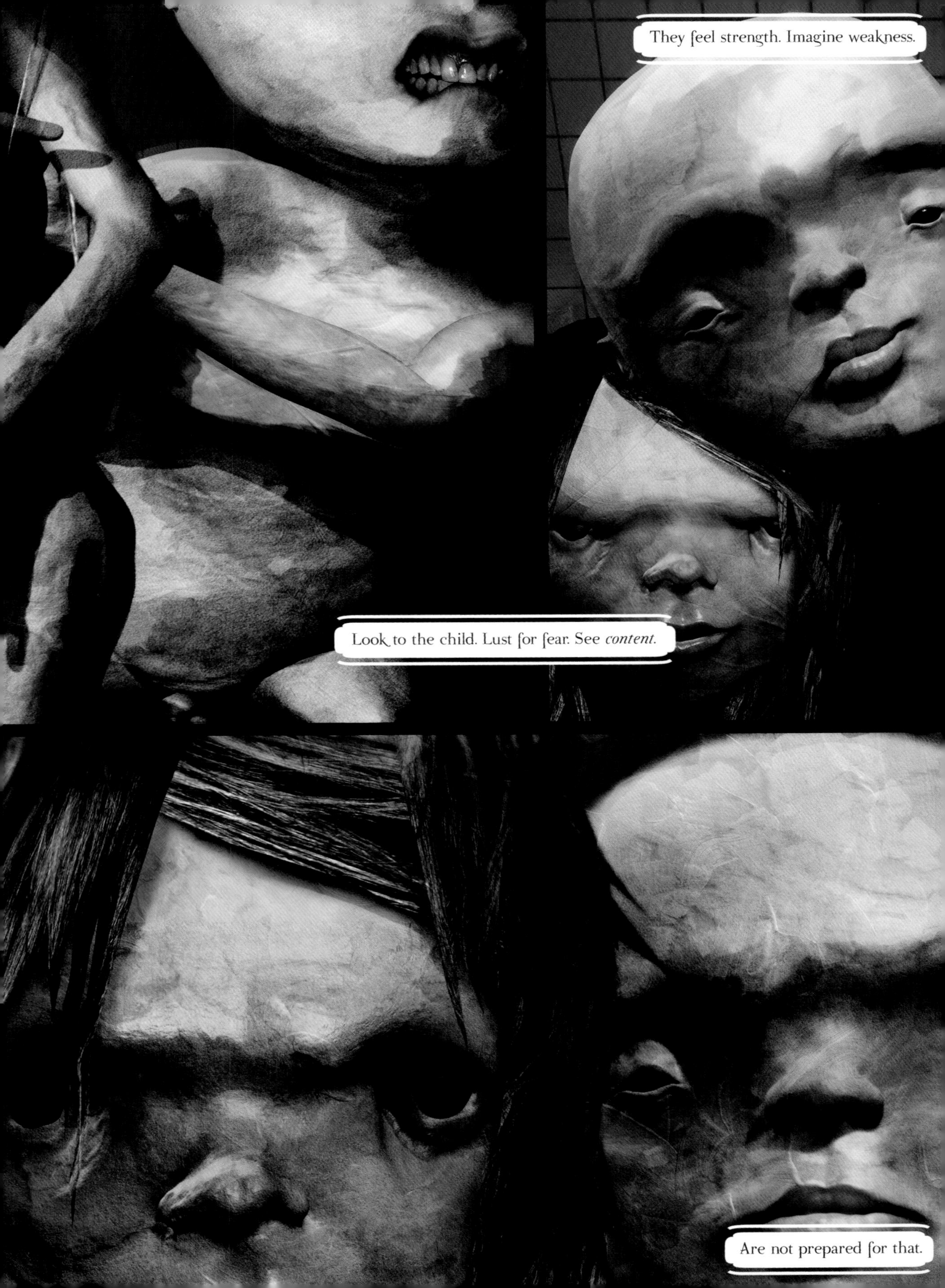
They feel strength. Imagine weakness.
Look to the child. Lust for fear. See *content.*
Are not prepared for that.

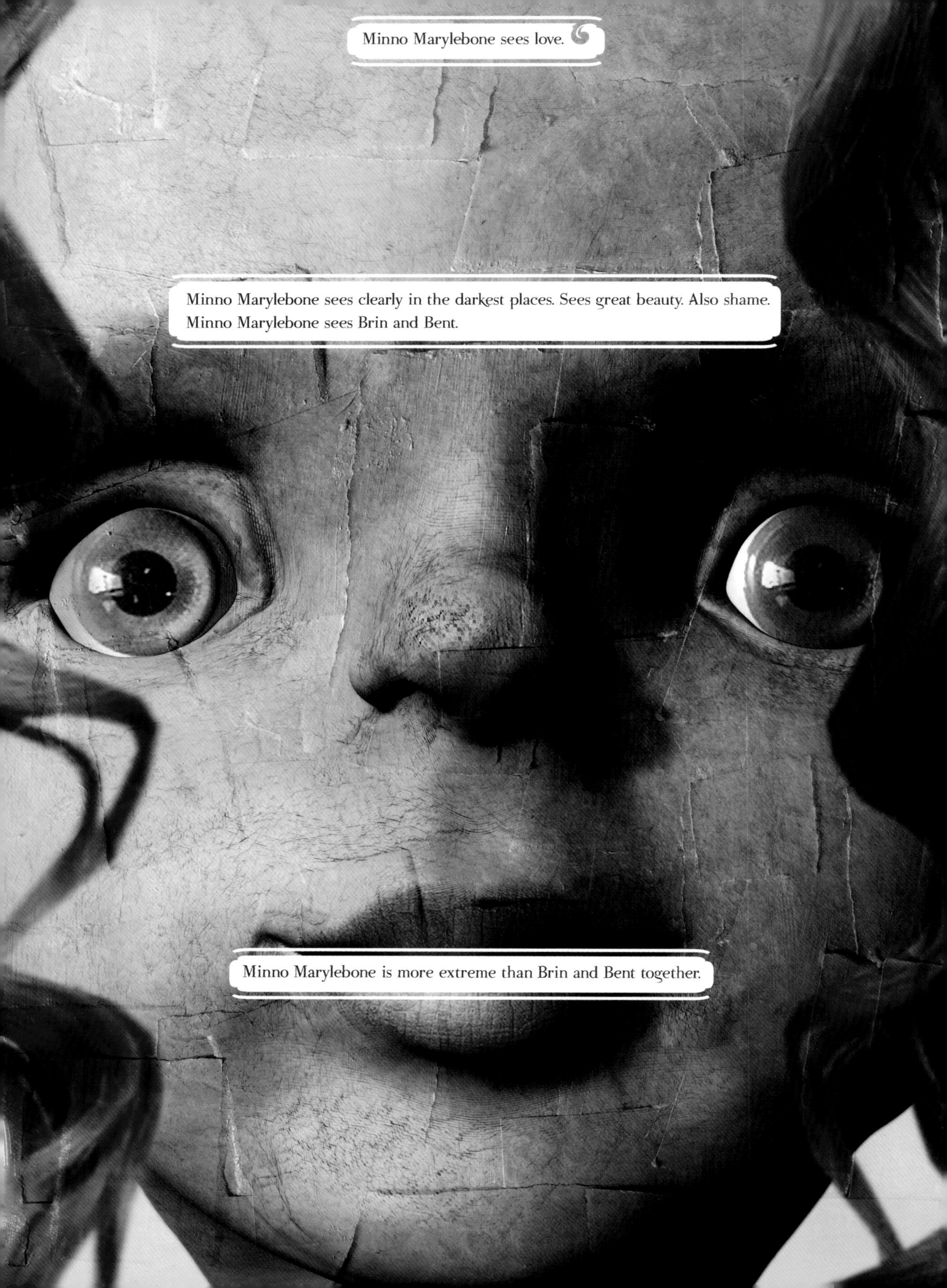
Minno Marylebone sees love.
Minno Marylebone sees clearly in the darkest places. Sees great beauty. Also shame. Minno Marylebone sees Brin and Bent.
Minno Marylebone is more extreme than Brin and Bent together.

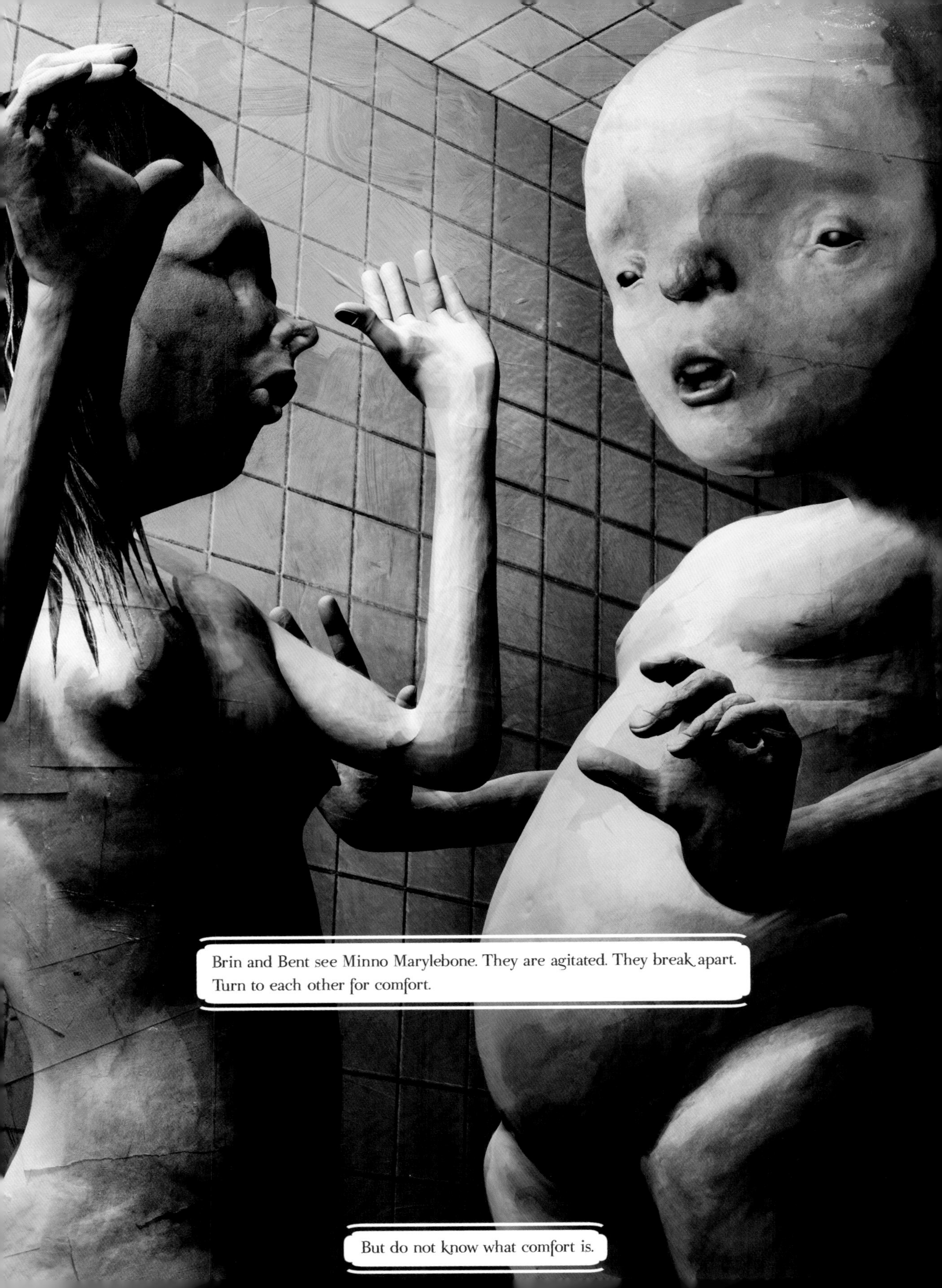
Brin and Bent see Minno Marylebone. They are agitated. They break apart. Turn to each other for comfort.
But do not know what comfort is.

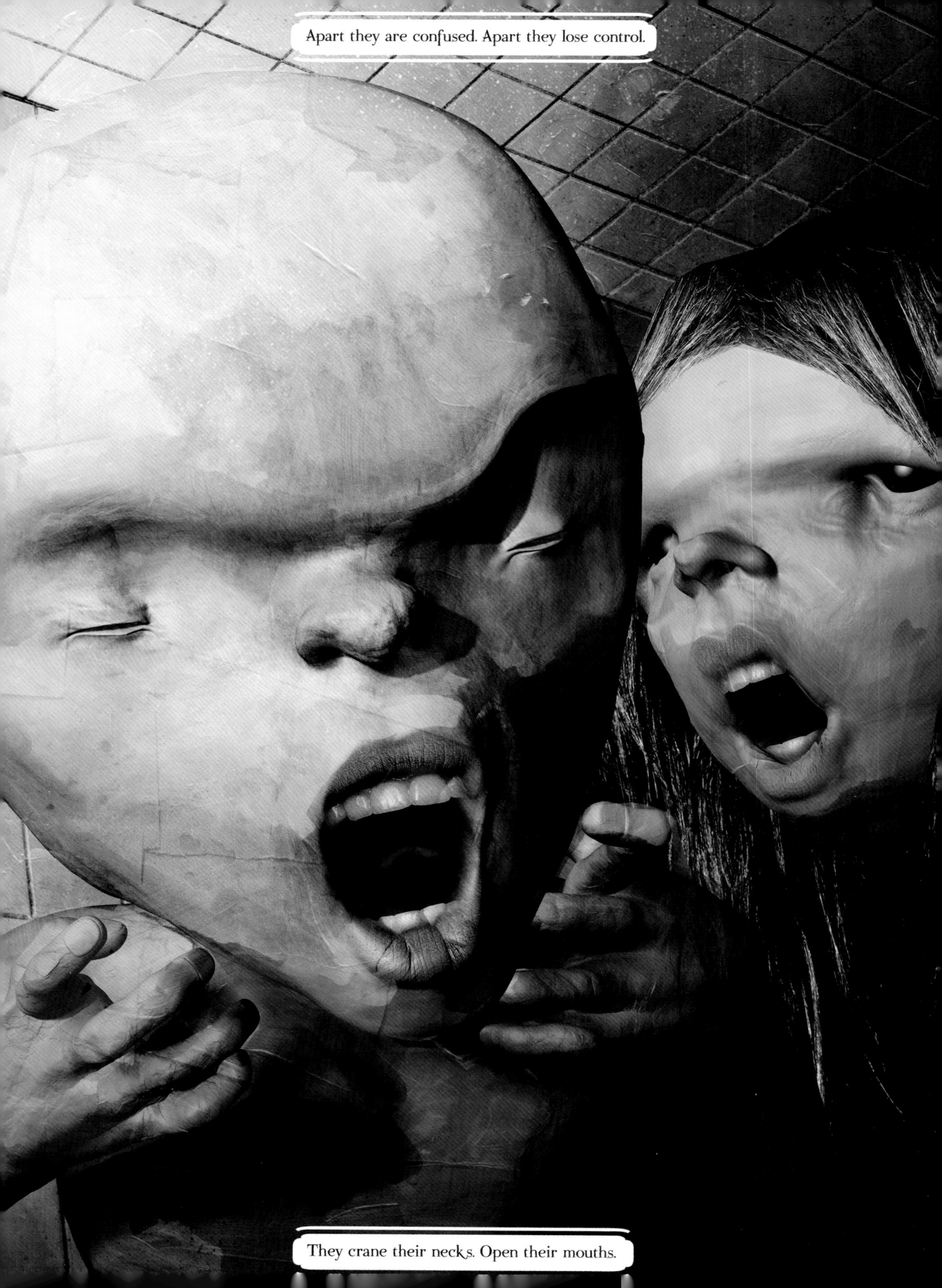
Apart they are confused. Apart they lose control.
They crane their necks. Open their mouths.

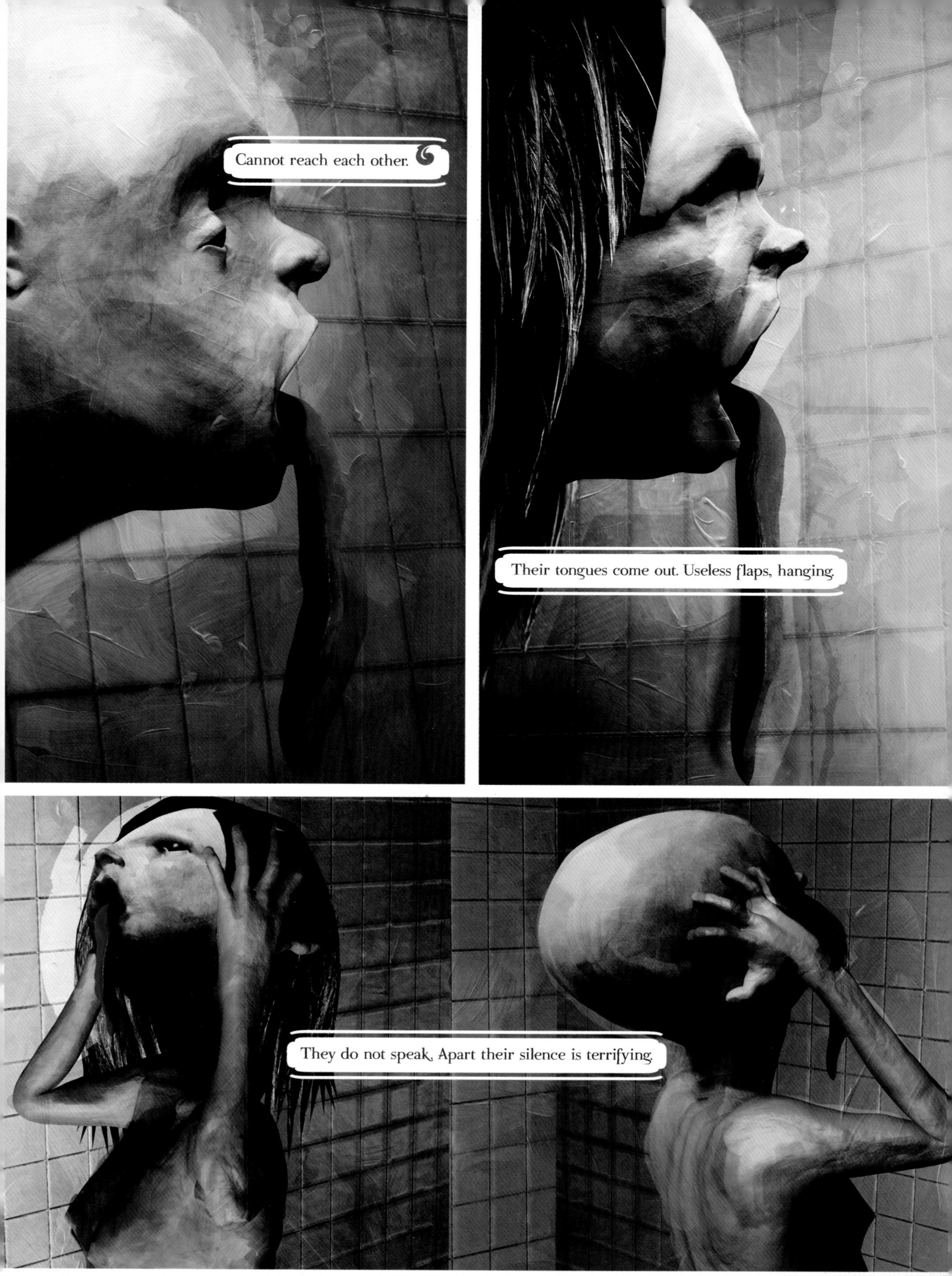
Cannot reach each other.
Their tongues come out. Useless flaps, hanging.
They do not speak. Apart their silence is terrifying.

They turn to the child. Tear at the gag. Reach for the mouth. Wanting words.
The possibility of speech. To be without fear.
Close to the child. Maws gaping, lolling.
Their breath is thick with their faces.

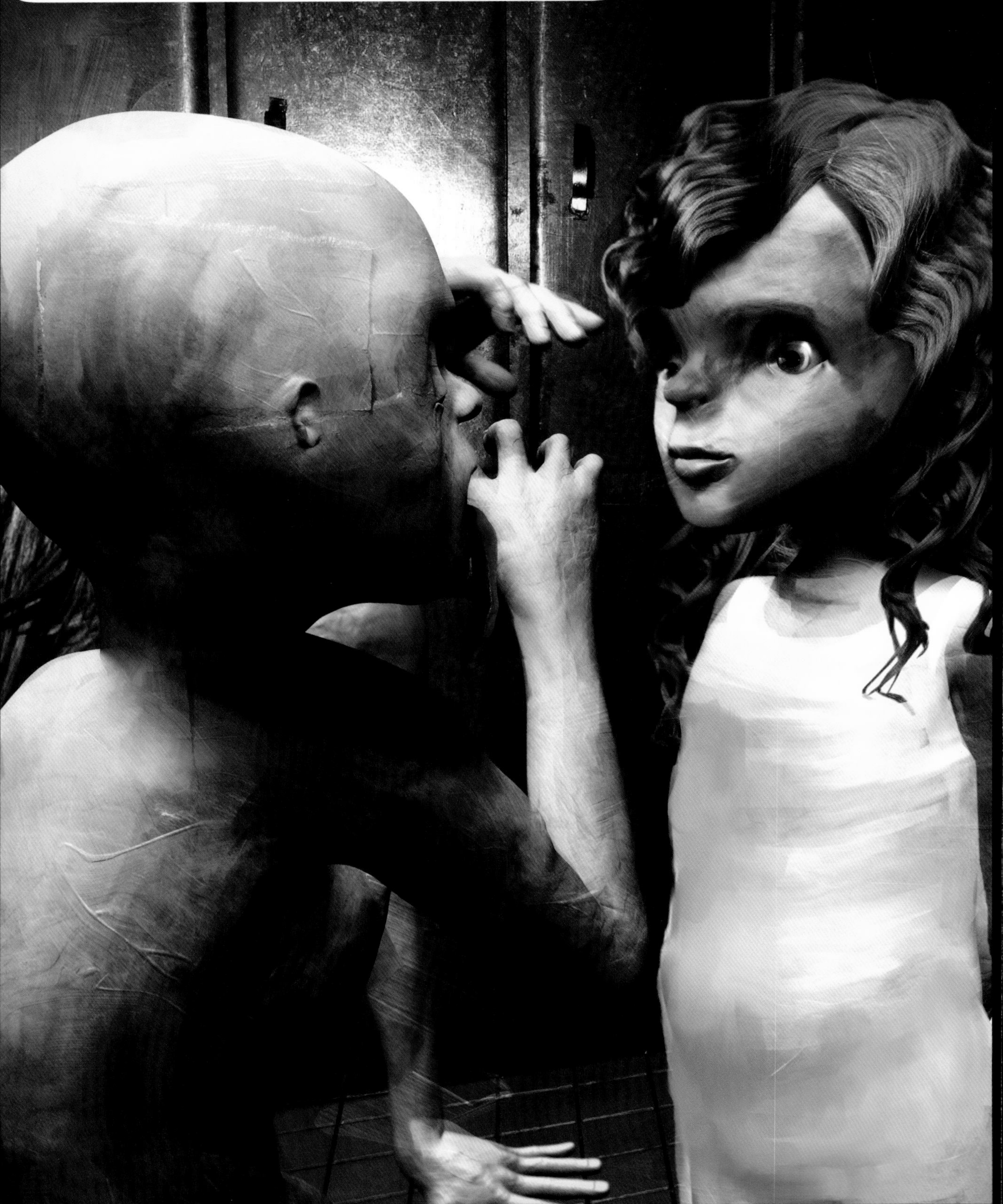

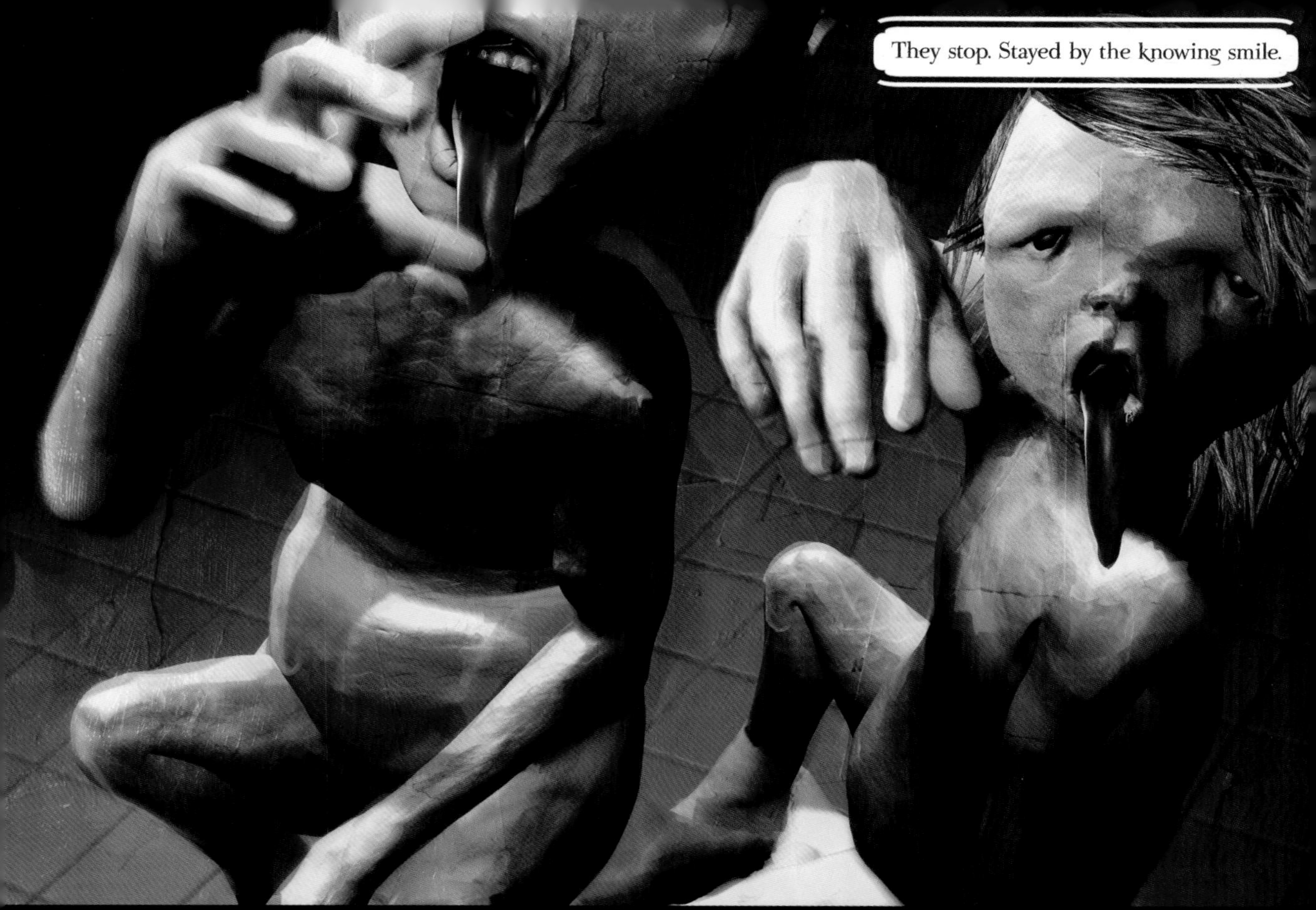
They stop. Stayed by the knowing smile.

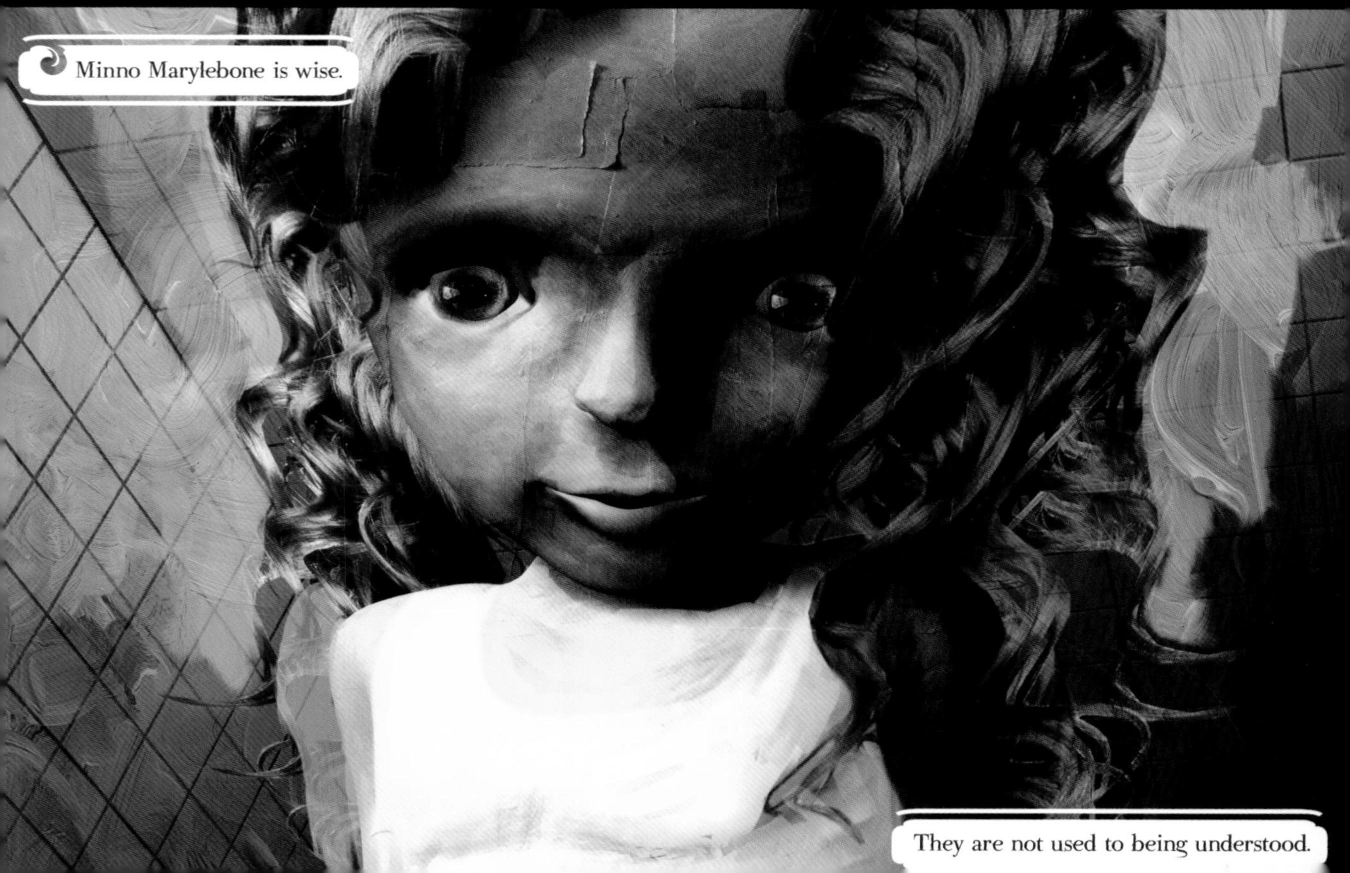
Minno Marylebone is wise.
They are not used to being understood.

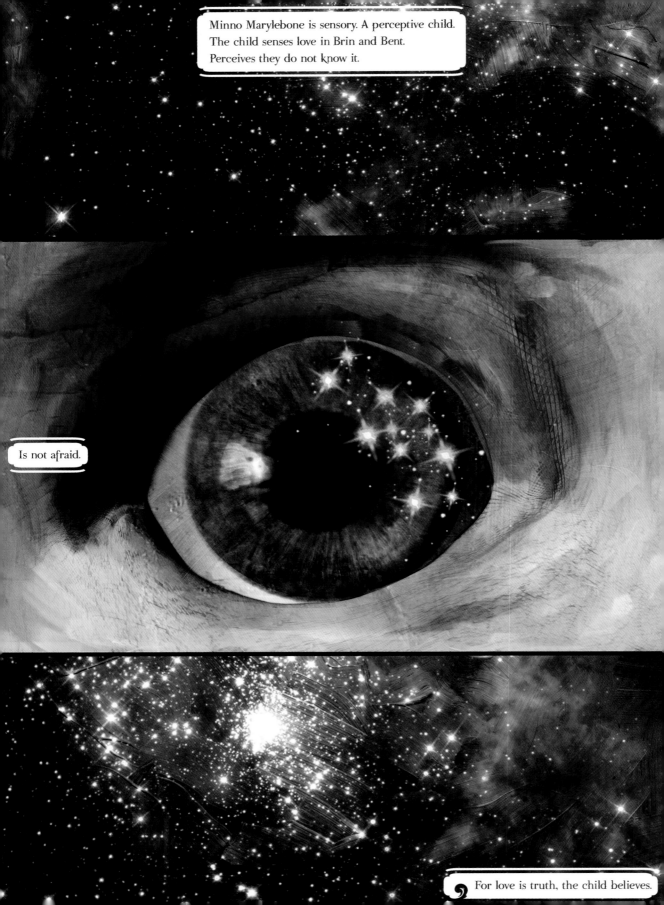

Minno Marylebone is sensory. A perceptive child.
The child senses love in Brin and Bent.
Perceives they do not know it.

Is not afraid.

For love is truth, the child believes.

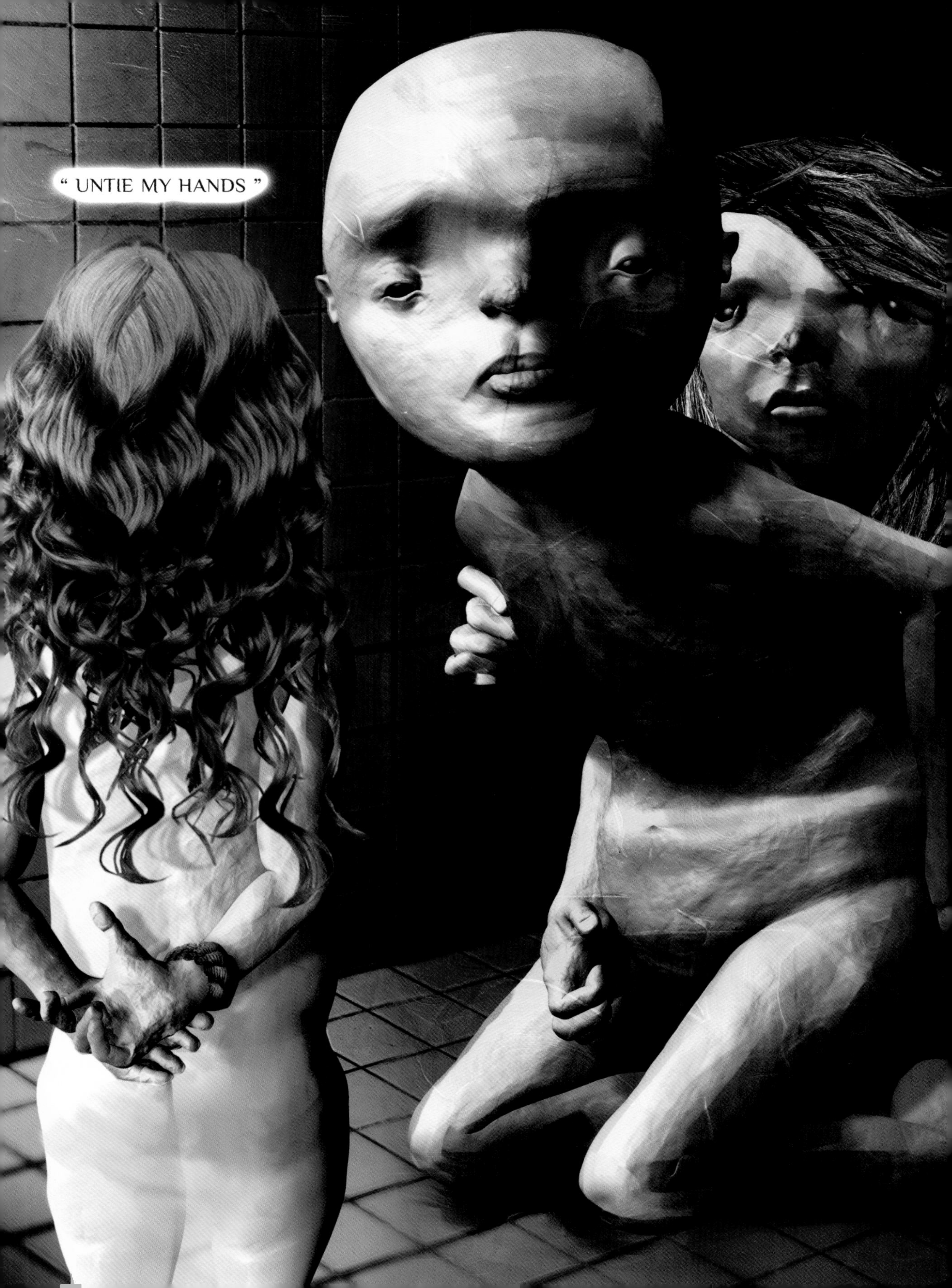
" UNTIE MY HANDS "

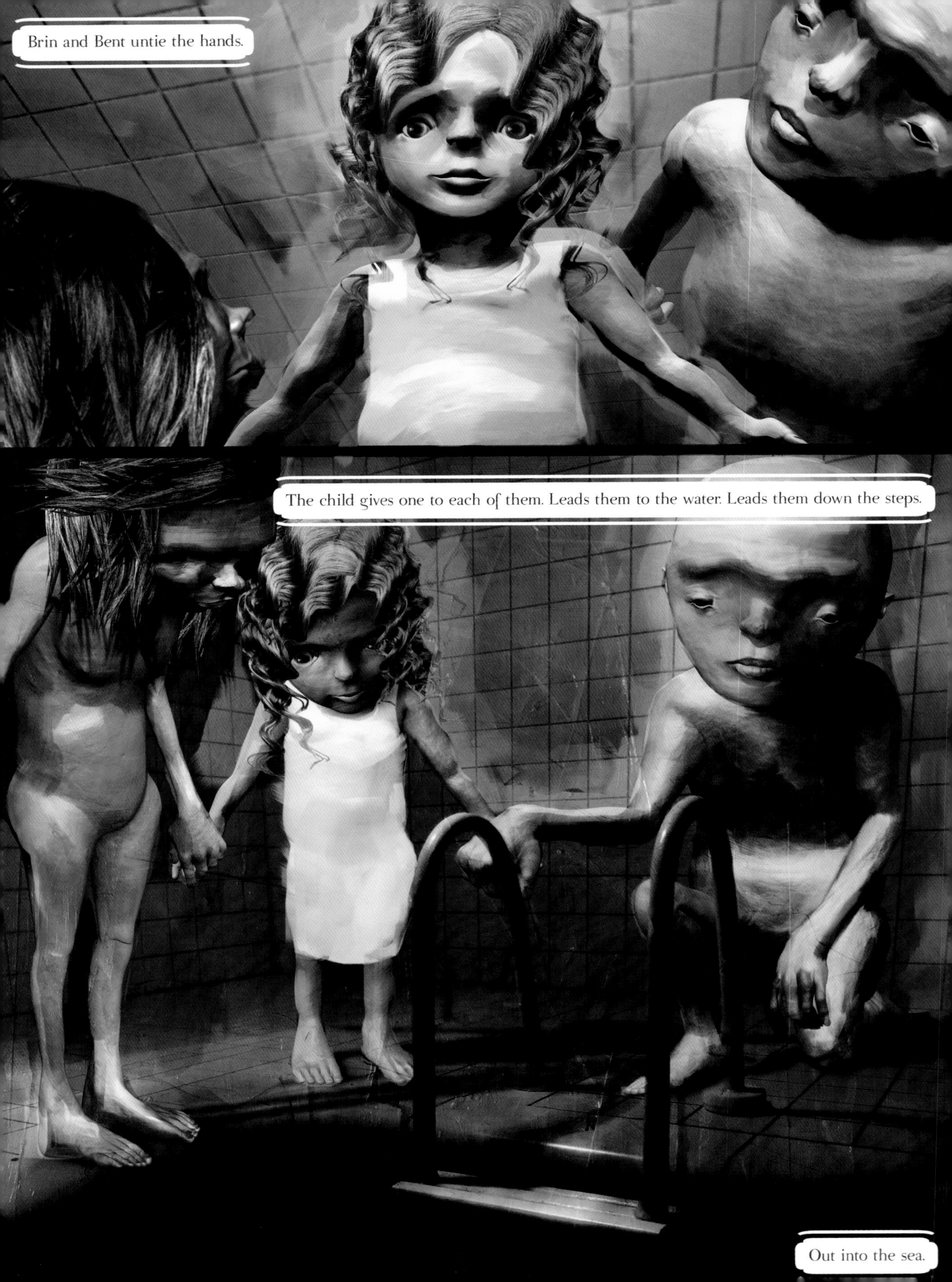
Brin and Bent untie the hands.
The child gives one to each of them. Leads them to the water. Leads them down the steps.
Out into the sea.

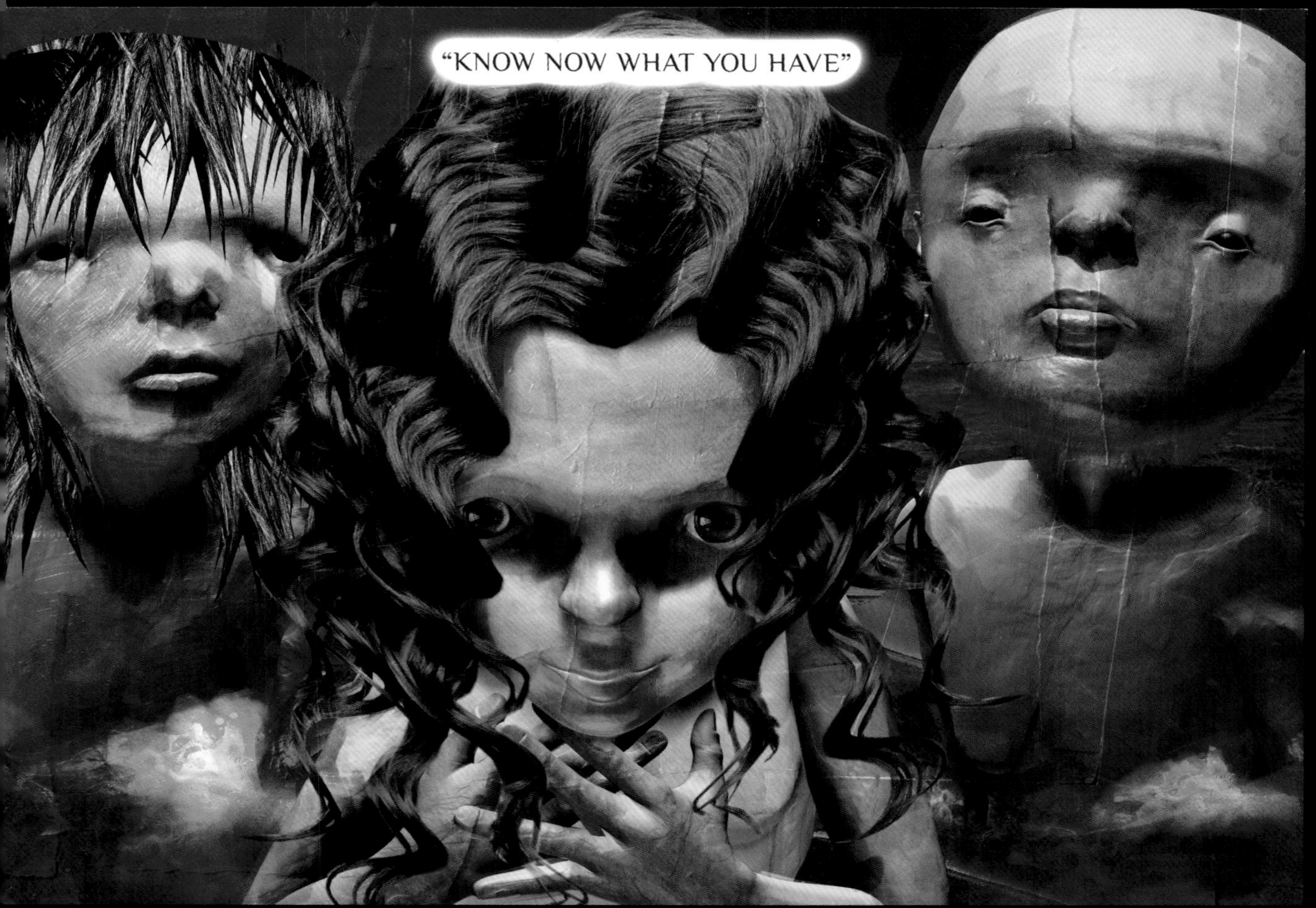
"KNOW NOW WHAT YOU HAVE"

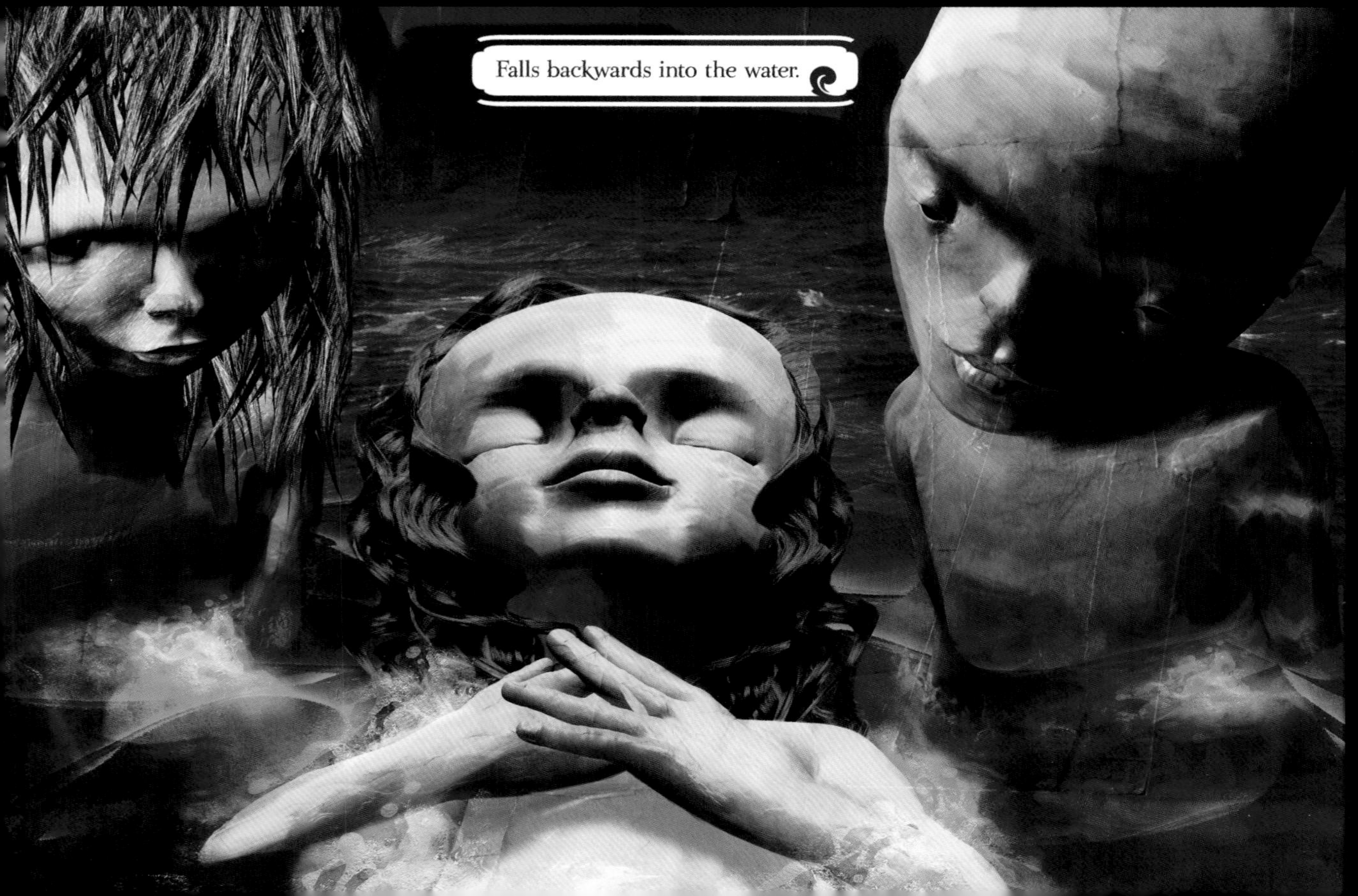
Falls backwards into the water.

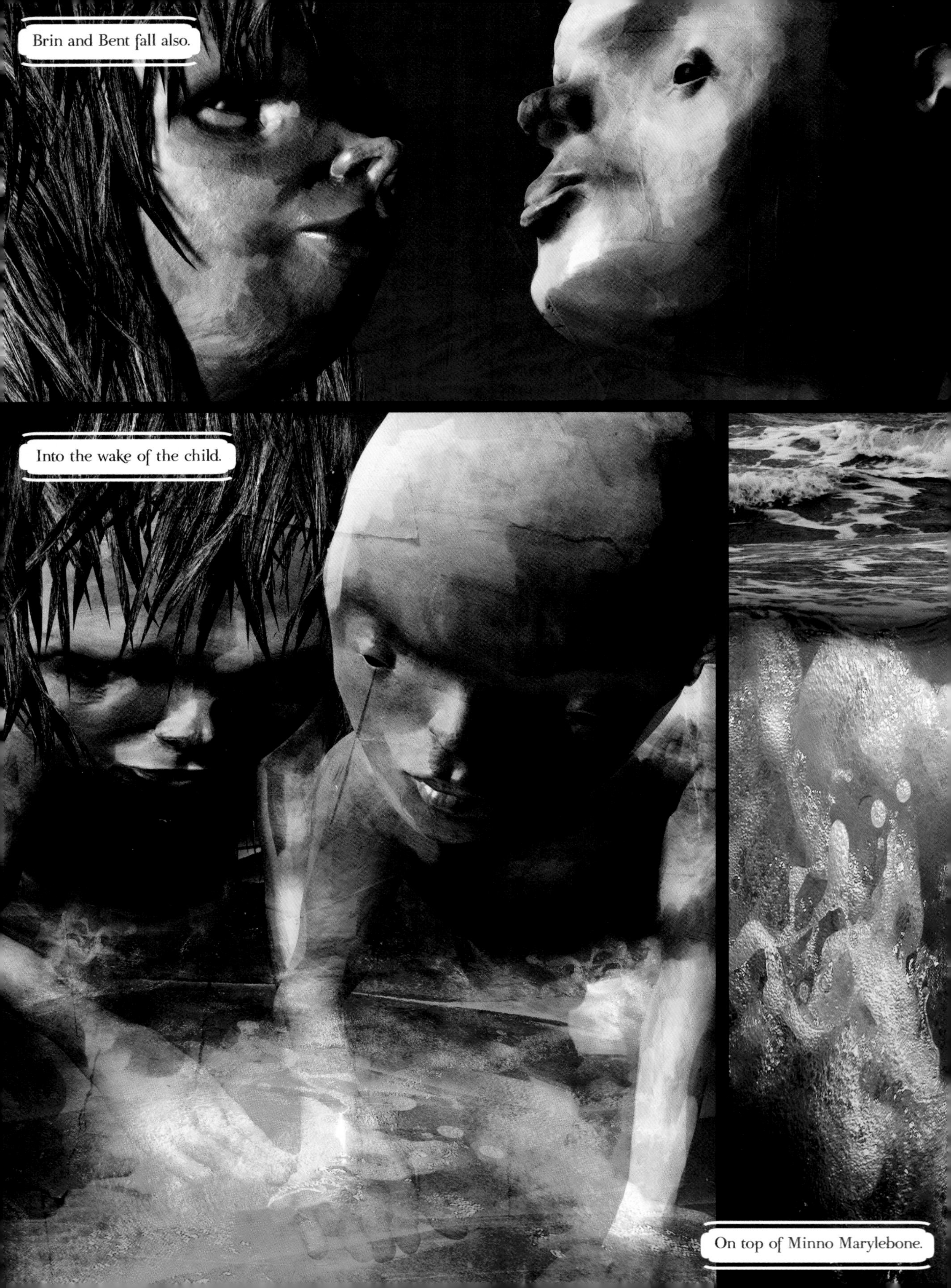
Brin and Bent fall also.
Into the wake of the child.
On top of Minno Marylebone.

The water darkens and stirs. A violent storm. Down go Brin and Bent on Minno Marylebone.

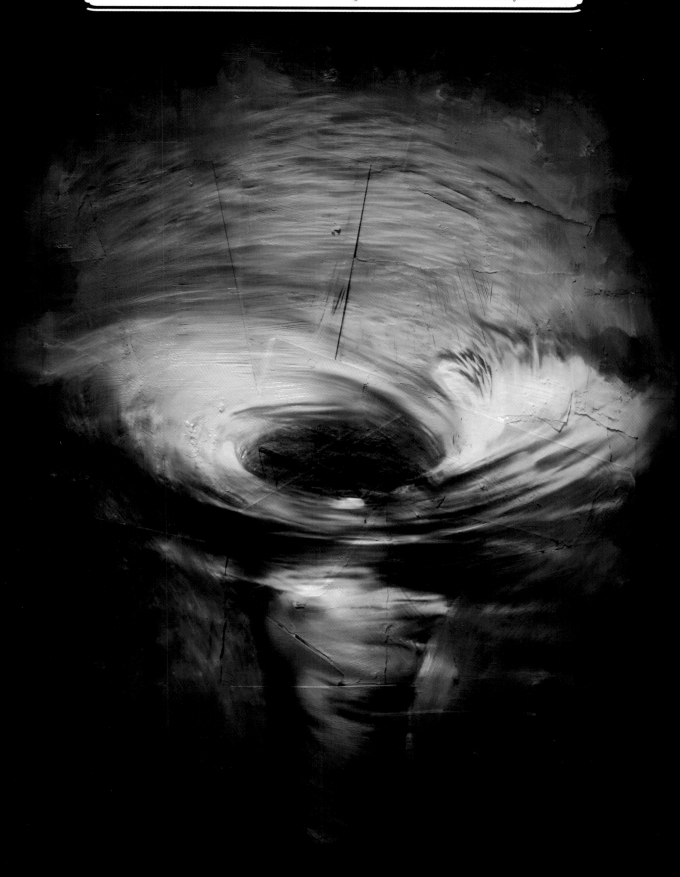

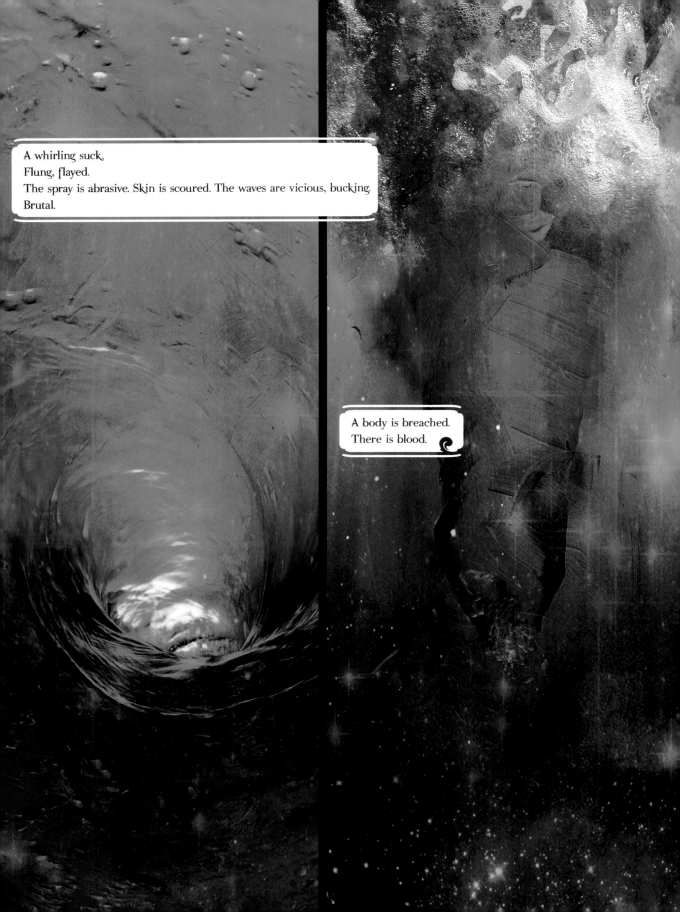

A whirling suck,
Flung, flayed.
The spray is abrasive. Skin is scoured. The waves are vicious, bucking,
Brutal.

A body is breached.
There is blood.

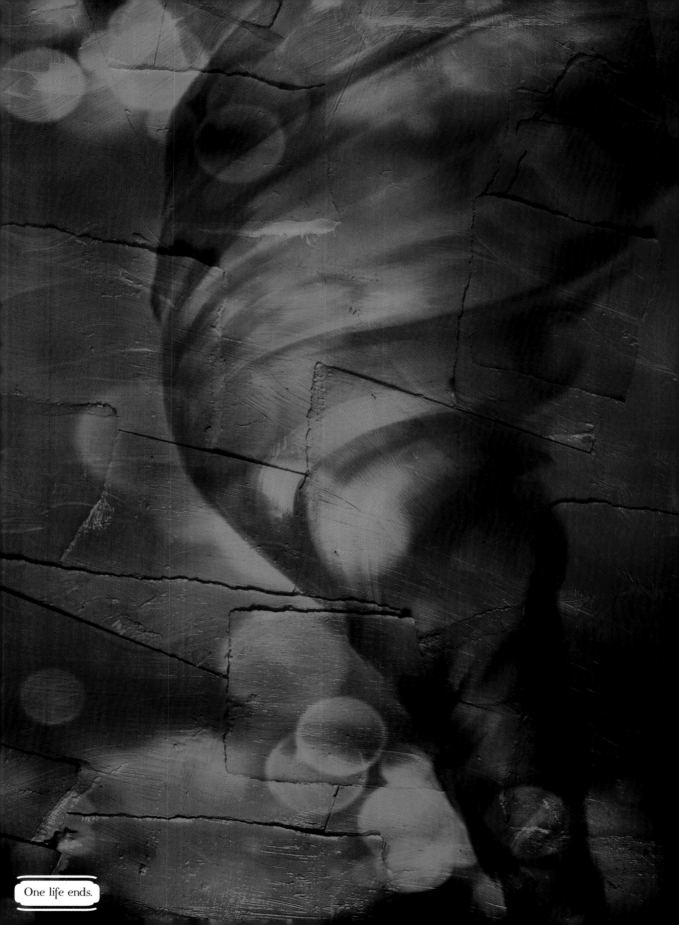

One life ends.

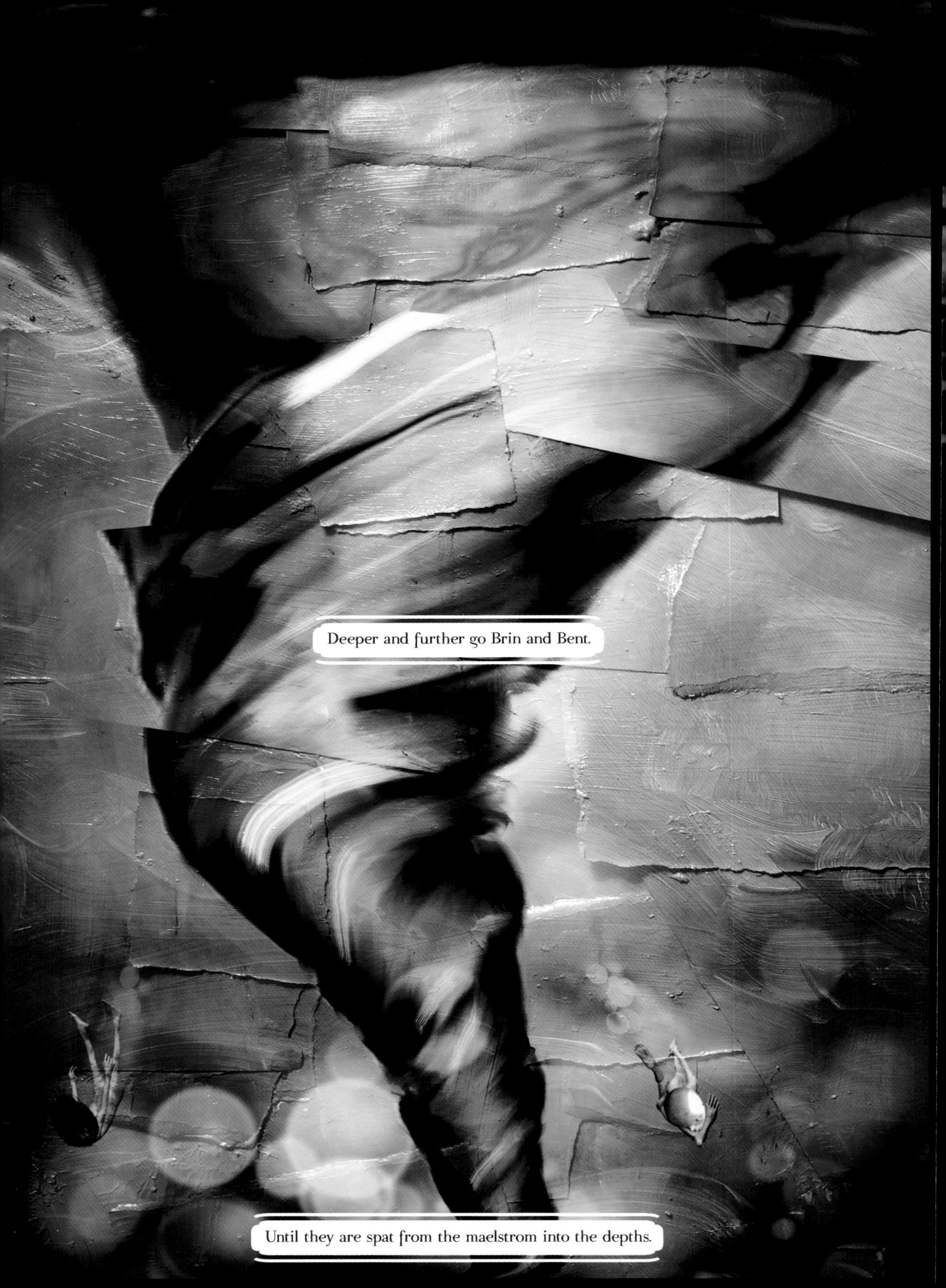
Deeper and further go Brin and Bent.
Until they are spat from the maelstrom into the depths.

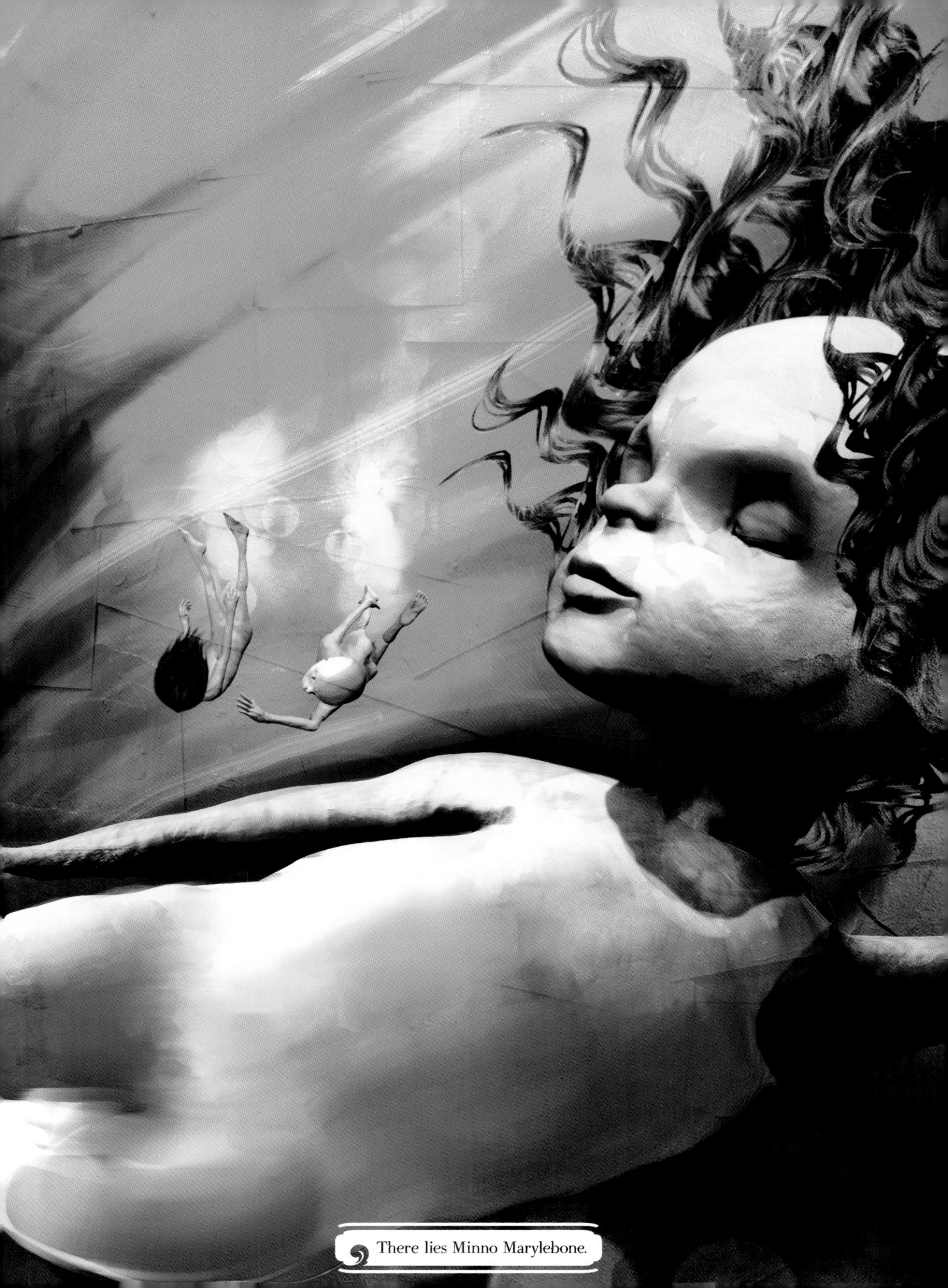

There lies Minno Marylebone.

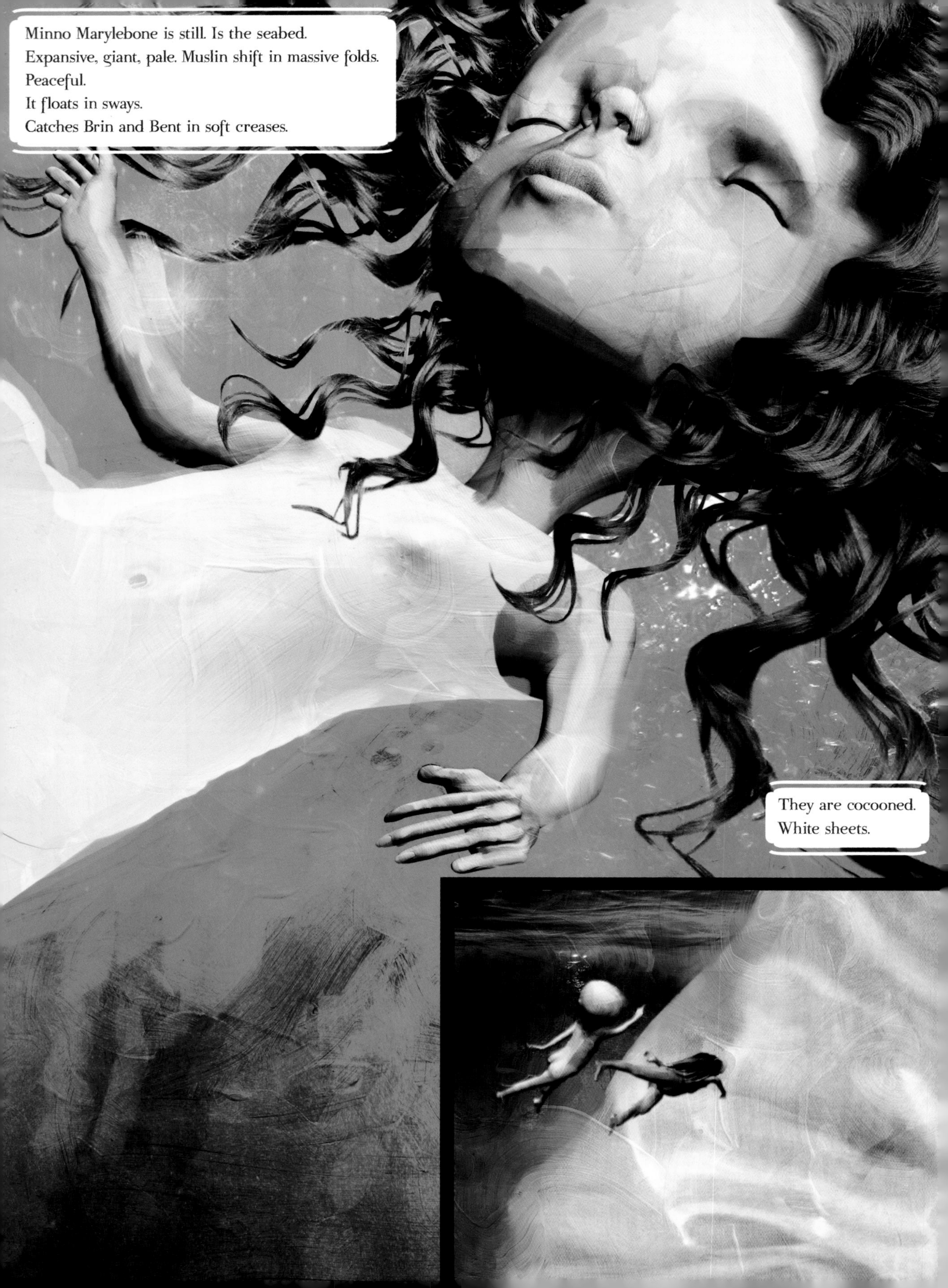
Minno Marylebone is still. Is the seabed.
Expansive, giant, pale. Muslin shift in massive folds.
Peaceful.
It floats in sways.
Catches Brin and Bent in soft creases.
They are cocooned.
White sheets.

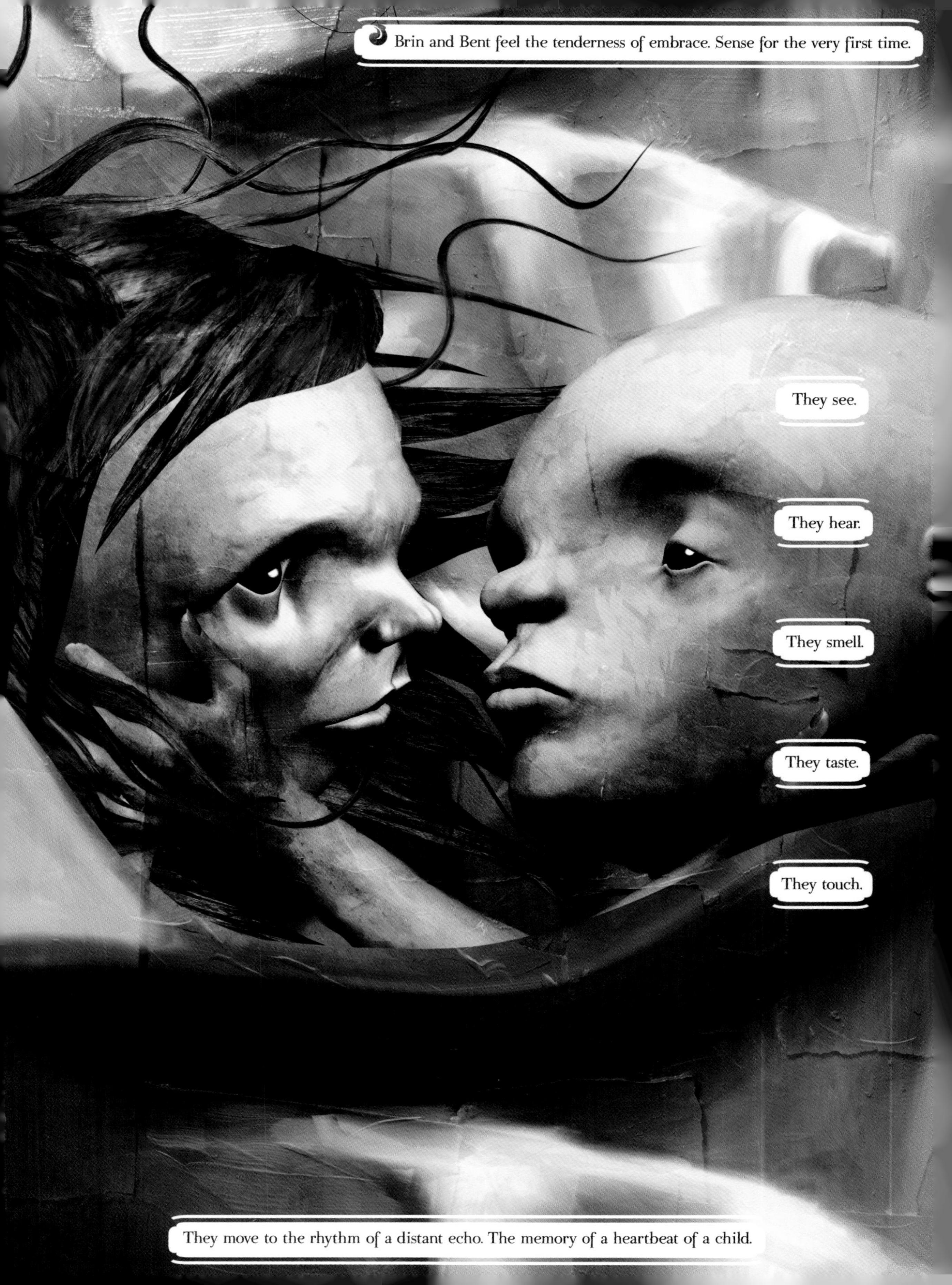
Brin and Bent feel the tenderness of embrace. Sense for the very first time.
They see.
They hear.
They smell.
They taste.
They touch.
They move to the rhythm of a distant echo. The memory of a heartbeat of a child.

Lovers. Brin and Bent on Minno Marylebone.

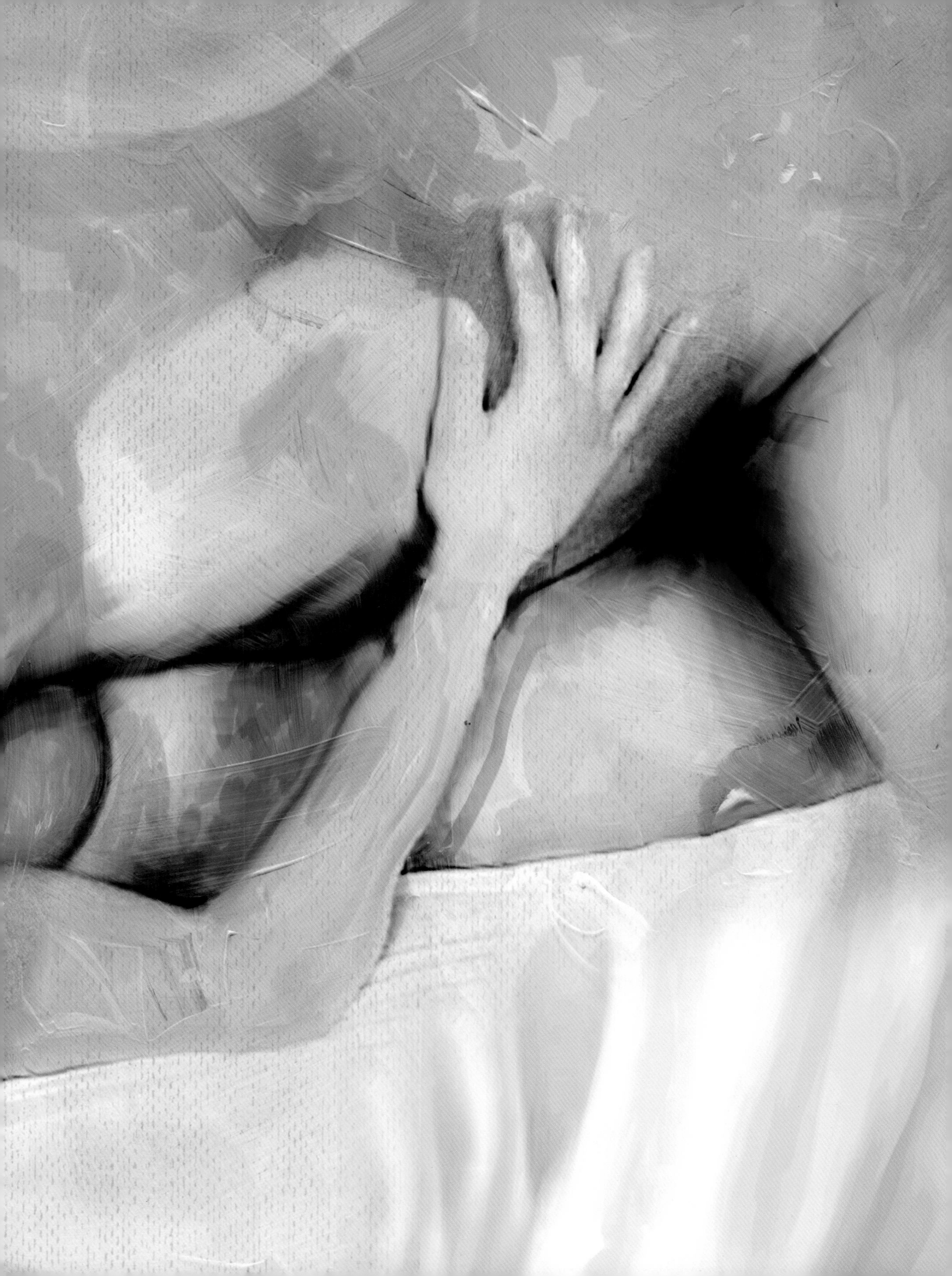

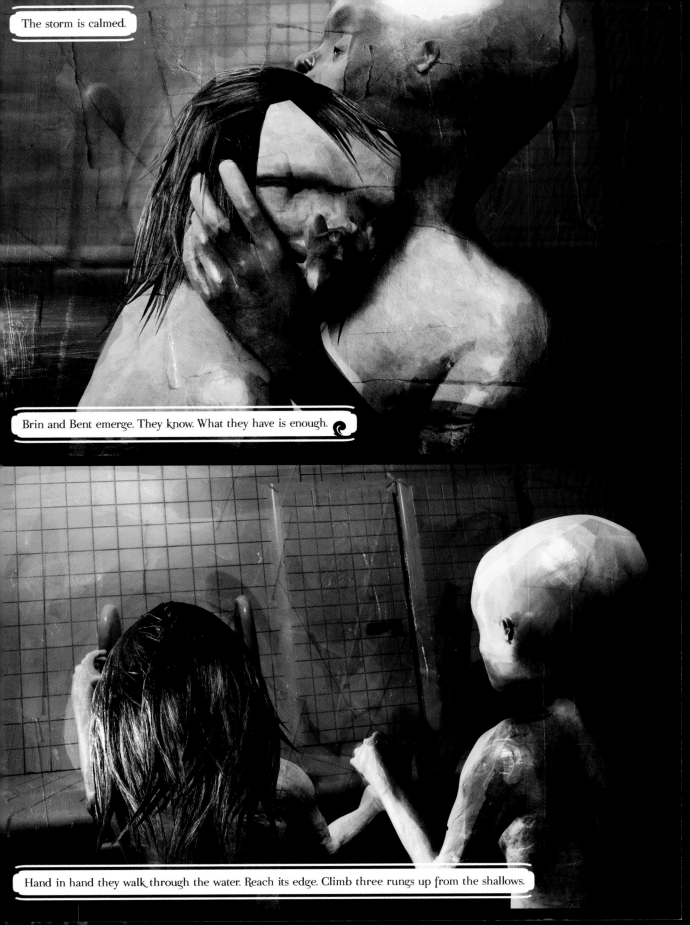

The storm is calmed.

Brin and Bent emerge. They know. What they have is enough.

Hand in hand they walk through the water. Reach its edge. Climb three rungs up from the shallows.

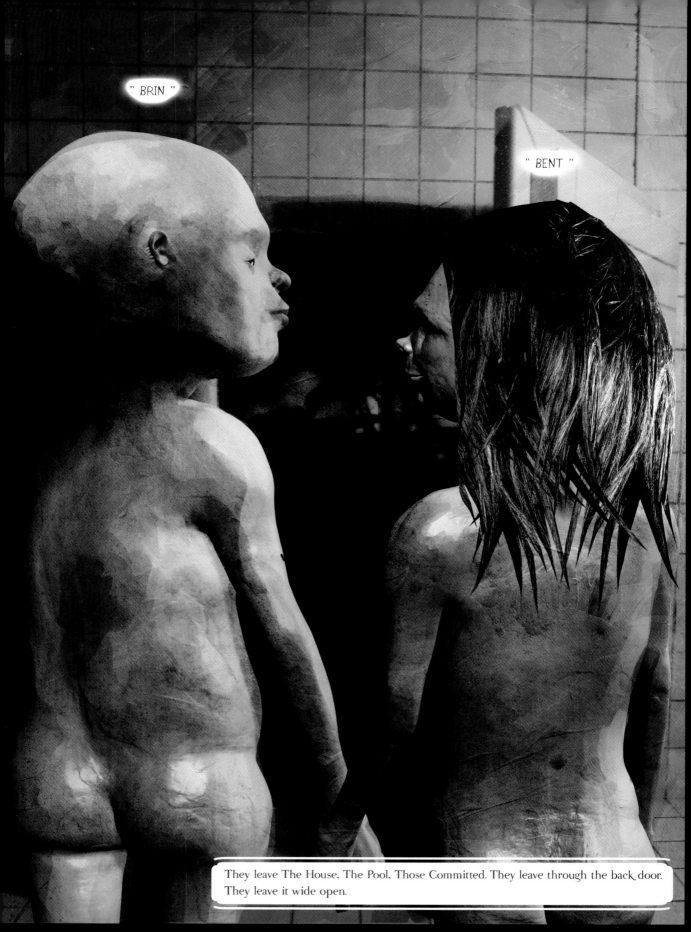

They leave The House, The Pool, Those Committed. They leave through the back door. They leave it wide open.

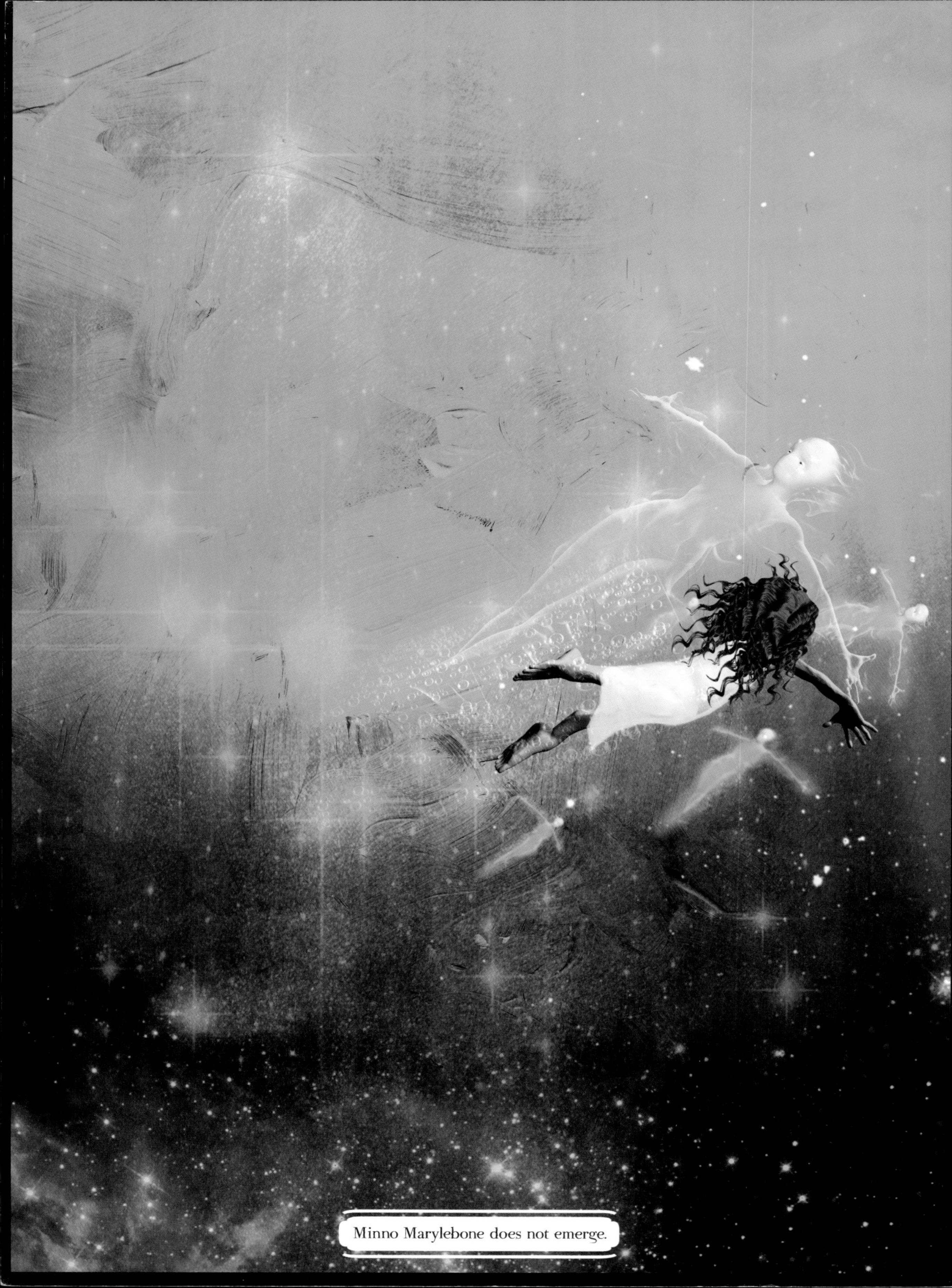
Minno Marylebone does not emerge.

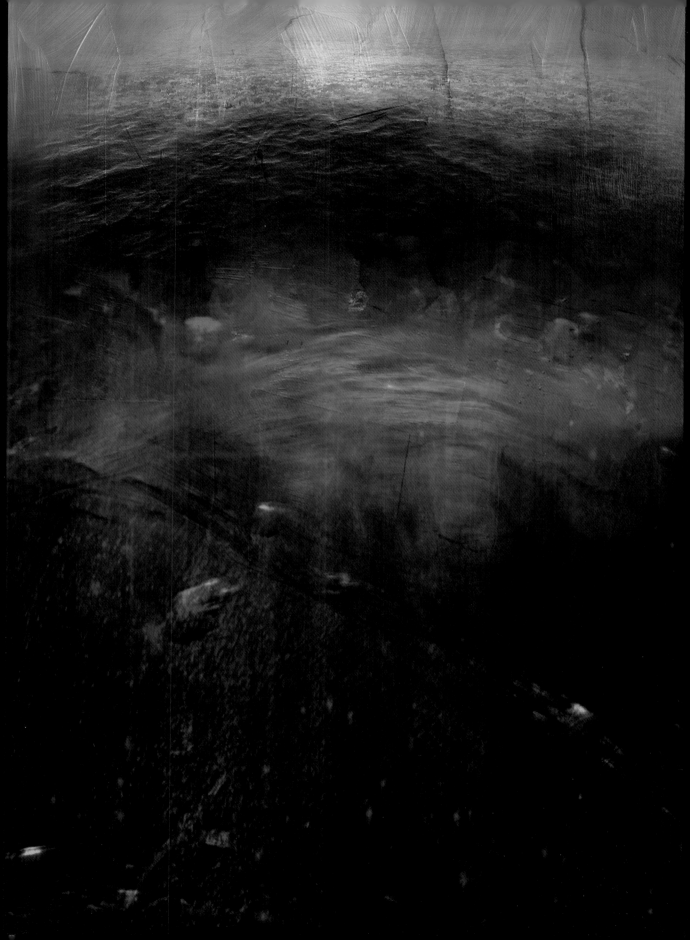

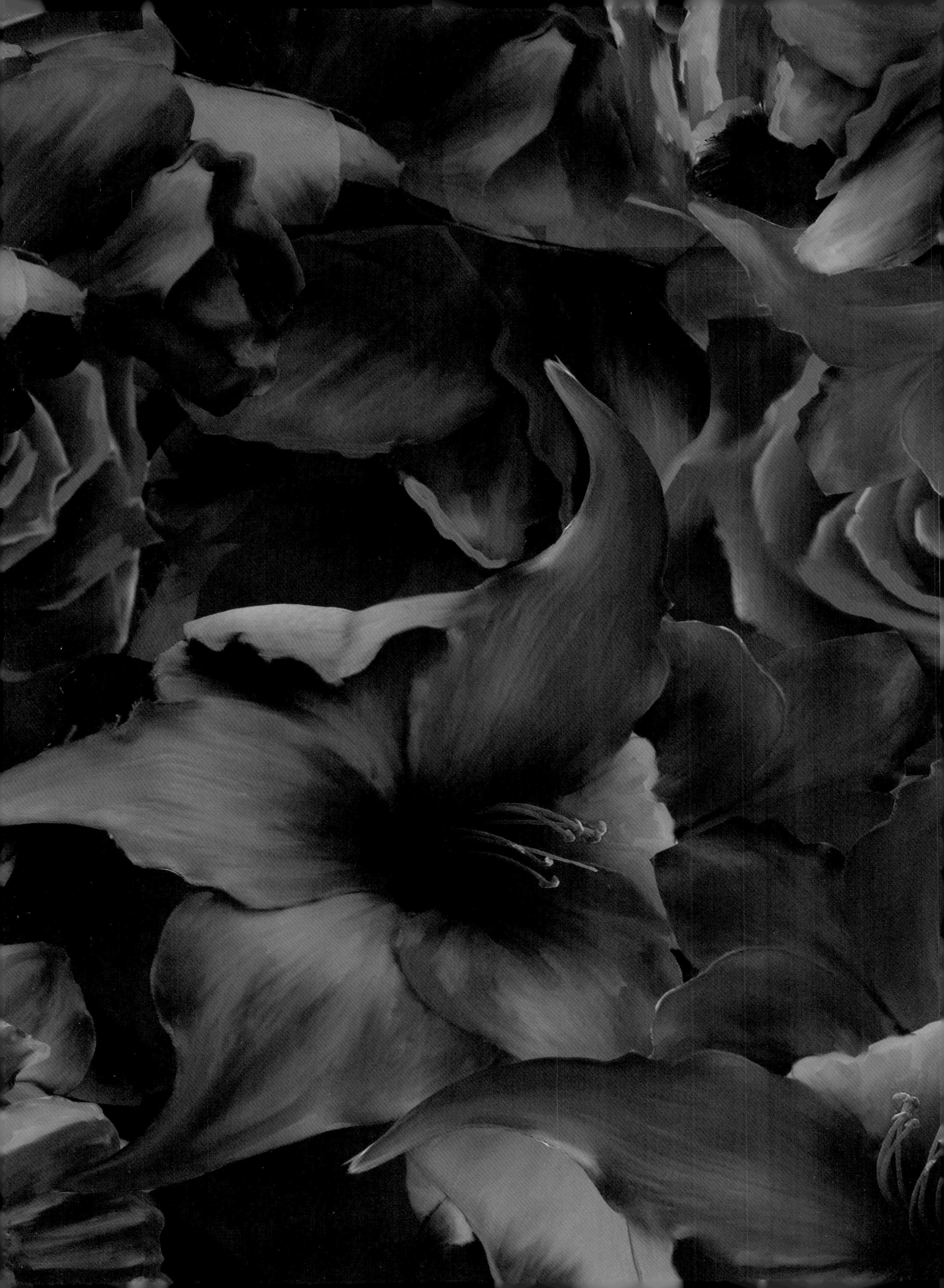

Ravi Thornton lives in Manchester with the Elegant Hound. The Tale of Brin & Bent and Minno Marylebone is her first graphic novel.

'Written in the blackest of hours, it took a long time for me to bring this tale into the light.

I'd like to thank all of those who helped me to move beyond the shadows of my past: the Inner Circle for their patience and unwavering belief; Andy Hixon for further illuminating dark corners; Othon Mataragas for his exquisite score.

This book is dedicated to the angel on my left shoulder and the ghost upon my right.'

www.ravithornton.com
@ravithornton on Twitter

Andy Hixon loves and taunts several people across the Manchester and Sheffield area.

He likes dark and twisted films, pug dogs and curry. He also likes working with clay, photography, digital media and animation. He can be found at www.andyhixon.com

'Much love and special thanks to: Ann, Rick and Chris Hixon, and a super special thanks to Kate for all her continued love and support.

Many thanks to Ravi for getting me involved in this amazing project and her continued friendship. To Ste Nuttall, Paul Roberts and Ben Jones, for being great friends and also damn good drinking buddies. To all the people involved at Jonathan Cape and Random House. And to Craig Fyfe for his disturbing drawings.'

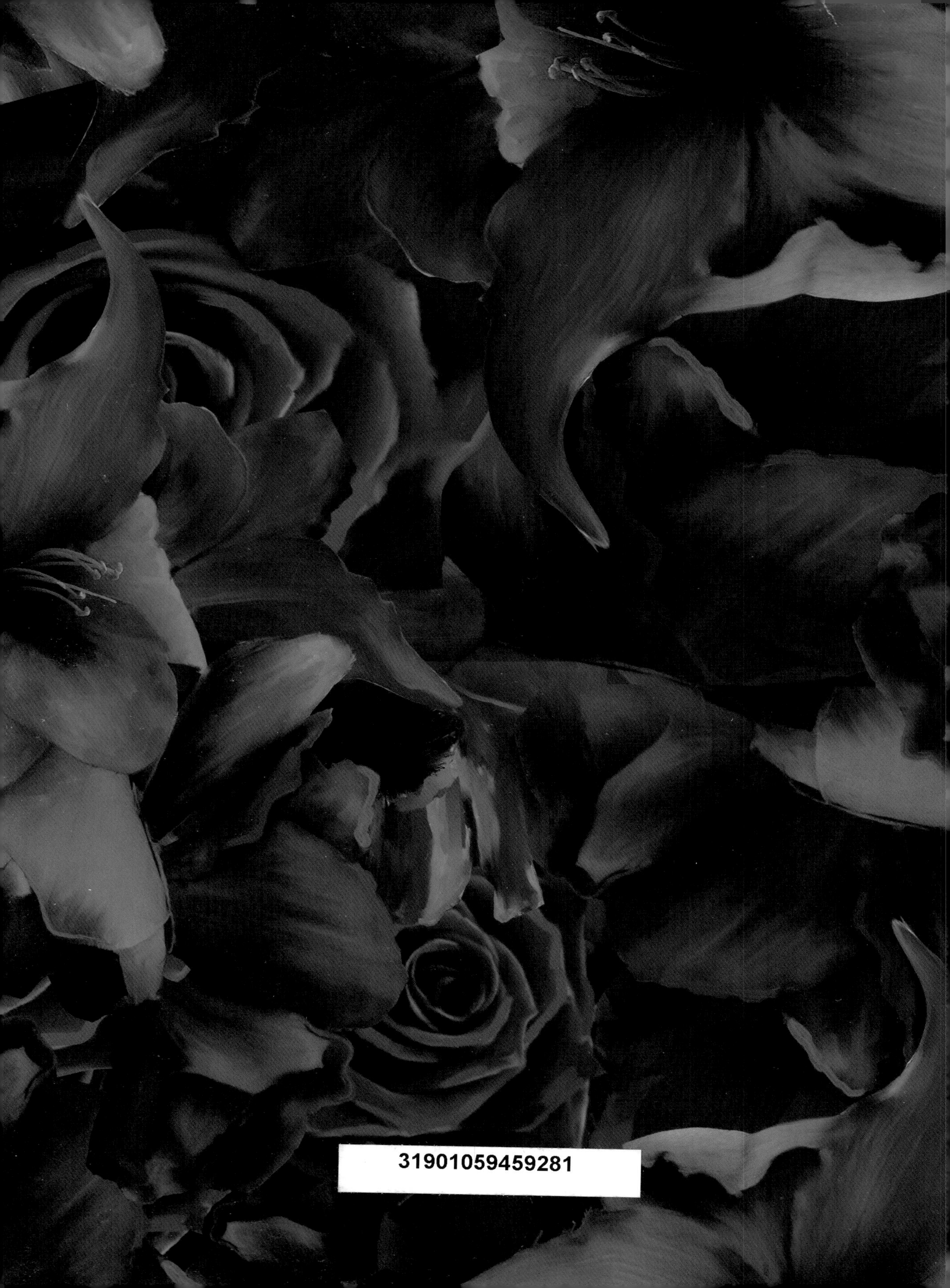